SPANISH ONCE A WEEK

By

NORMA CLEGG, A.I.L.

and

PATRICIA K. CALDWELL, F.I.L.

General Editor:

P. H. HARGREAVES, B.A., F.I.L.

BASIL BLACKWELL · OXFORD

ALSO IN THIS SERIES

GERMAN ONCE A WEEK, BOOKS I and II
FRENCH ONCE A WEEK, BOOKS I and II
SALUT LA FRANCE!

0 631 94610 1

Made in Great Britain at the Pitman Press, Bath

AUTHORS' NOTE

Spanish Once A Week, like its French and German counterparts, is designed first and foremost for use in evening classes by adult students wishing to acquire speedily a practical knowledge of the language. In addition, it will be found effective as a preliminary textbook for secondary school pupils preparing for examinations.

The twenty lessons centre round a coach tour based on Madrid, thus introducing the student to the enormously interesting region of Castile.

The vocabulary is restricted to a little under 1,000 common words and idiomatic expressions, including many cognates. Bold type in the text refers the student to the short vocabulary list in each lesson, while complete Spanish-English and English-Spanish vocabularies at the back eliminate the need for a dictionary at this early stage.

Without over-burdening the beginner with intricate grammatical details, *Spanish Once A Week* gives a thorough grounding in verb forms in the present, imperative and past, and deals clearly with the essentials of pronunciation, gender, number, comparison and agreement.

Our grateful thanks are due to Sra. D. Angeles Moro Muñoz of Madrid for her work in checking and revising the text.

P. K. C.
N. C.

CONTENTS

PRONUNCIATION AND STRESS

The Spanish Alphabet

a b c ch d e f g h i (latina) j l ll m
n ñ o p q r rr s t u v x y (griega) z
28 letters, excluding k and w; including ch, ll, ñ and rr.

The Vowels

a = a as in cat

e $\Big\langle$ short e as in get
long ei as in veil

i and y = ee as in teeth

o $\Big\langle$ short o as in got
long o as in go

u = oo in loop

There are no diphthongs. When two or more vowels follow one another each is pronounced separately.

The Consonants

b ch f l m n p t and y are pronounced as in English.

c $\Big\langle$ before a, o, u = k
before e, i = th as in thin

d $\Big\langle$ at the beginning of a syllable = d
at the end of a syllable = th as in thin, lightly; similarly between vowels

g $\Big\langle$ before a, o, u = g as in go
before e, i = a very hard h

h   is always silent

j   is a very hard h

ll = l + y as in colliery

ñ = n + y as in canyon

q   followed by u = k, used only before e, i

r   is slightly rolled

rr   is rolled twice as long as r

s = ss

v = b

x $\begin{cases} \text{between two vowels} = x \\ \text{between a vowel and a consonant} = ss \end{cases}$

z = th as in thin, rarely used before e, i

Rules for Stress

1. Words ending in a vowel or n or s take the stress on next to the last syllable, e.g. pat**a**ta, **en**tran.
2. Words ending in a consonant, except n or s, take the stress on the last syllable, e.g. ed**ad**, rel**oj**.
3. Exceptions to rules 1 and 2 bear an accent on the stressed syllable, e.g. pasó, útil, rápido.
4. Two strong vowels, i.e. a, e, o count as two syllables, e.g. pa/se/o, while any other pair of vowels counts as only one syllable, e.g. ciu/dad, mue/bles, Ma/ría.
5. Capital letters do not have accents.

SPANISH ONCE A WEEK

LECCION 1

ESTAMOS EN MADRID

El grupo inglés está en el **autocar**. El autocar pasa por Francia y el norte de España y está en Madrid, capital de España. Madrid está en el centro de España. El grupo inglés está en el Hotel Santo Domingo en el centro de la capital. El hotel es elegante. Muchas personas están en el autocar; Bill, **el conductor**, Robert, **el guía** y los pasajeros.

Bill **dice**—Soy el conductor.

Robert dice—Soy el guía. Somos de la Agencia 'Sunnidays'.

Los pasajeros son:

La familia Brown. El señor Brown es arquitecto.

La familia Reilly. El señor Reilly es dentista.

La familia Scott. El señor Scott es médico.

La familia Evans. El señor Evans es profesor.

Dos (2) futbolistas.

Cuatro (4) profesoras.

Seis (6) estudiantes.

Diez (10) **matrimonios.**

El grupo está muy contento **porque** el hotel es elegante. ¡El conductor y el guía están contentos porque los pasajeros están contentos!

En el hotel, Robert distribuye la lista de excursiones. La lista es interesante.

Día uno (1)   Madrid

Día dos (2)   Toledo

Día tres (3)   Madrid: Museo del Prado y el Retiro

Día cuatro (4)   Aranjuez

Día cinco (5)   El Escorial

Día seis (6)   Madrid: La Moncloa

Día siete (7)   Avila

Día ocho (8)   Madrid: Corrida de Toros

Día nueve (9)   Segovia
Día diez (10)   Madrid: Sala de Fiestas
—La lista es magnífica—dice el señor Evans.
—Sí, señor Evans, es muy interesante—dice el doctor Scott.
—¡Es fantástico!—dice el señor Reilly.
—Y el hotel es fantástico—dice el señor Brown. —Estoy muy contento.
—Sí, estamos muy contentos—dice la señora Brown.

VOCABULARIO

el autocar	the coach
el conductor	the driver
el guía	the guide
el matrimonio	the married couple
dice	says
porque	because

GRAMATICA

1. **Gender.** Objects as well as living things are divided into masculine and feminine. For instance, a hotel is *he* while a house is *she*. The only foolproof way of knowing whether a noun is masculine or feminine is to learn it with its definite article.
2. **The Definite Article.** In the singular the masculine form of *the* is **el** and the feminine form is **la**.

Examples:

Masculine		*Feminine*	
el hotel	the hotel	la agencia	the agency
el grupo	the group	la capital	the capital
el centro	the centre	la familia	the family

It is useful to know that nouns ending in **-o** are generally masculine while those ending in **-a** are generally feminine, but there are exceptions. Note, el dentista, el futbolista.

Note :

   Bill es **el** conductor. Bill is *the* driver. (a particular driver)
but Bill es conductor. Bill is *a* driver. (his job)

3. **Señor, señora.** Notice that when speaking TO a person
   you say señor Evans—Mr. Evans *and* señora Evans—Mrs.
   Evans, but when speaking ABOUT a person you say **el
   señor Evans, la señora Evans.**

4. **Omission of Subject Pronouns.** These are generally
   omitted in both spoken and written Spanish because the
   varying verb endings make them superfluous. They can,
   however, be used to avoid confusion, e.g. in the 3rd person,
   and for emphasis.

5. **Two Verbs 'to be'.** Spanish has two verbs, **ser** and **estar,**
   which in different circumstances mean *to be.*

	Ser	**Estar**	
(yo)	soy	estoy	I am
(tú)	eres	estás	you are (familiar, singular)
(él)	es	está	he is, it is
(ella)	es	está	she is, it is
(Vd.)	es	está	you are (polite, singular)
(nosotros-as)	somos	estamos	we are
(vosotros-as)	sois	estáis	you are (familiar, plural)
(ellos, ellas)	son	están	they are
(Vds.)	son	están	you are (polite, plural)

For learning by heart, each verb can be reduced to four or
six words depending on whether or not you wish to learn
the familiar forms.

Ser	**Estar**
soy	estoy
eres	estás
es	está
somos	estamos
sois	estáis
son	están

It is essential from the start to learn the different uses of
ser and **estar.**

Ser indicates WHO and WHAT, i.e. identity, nationality, permanent and inherent characteristics and occupation.

Examples:

El señor Brown es inglés.   Mr. Brown is English.
Bill es el conductor.   Bill is the driver.
El señor Evans es inteligente. Mr. Evans is clever.

Estar indicates WHERE and HOW, i.e. position, condition and temporary state.

Examples:

Robert y Bill están en el   Robert and Bill are in
  autocar.   the coach.
La señora Scott está contenta. Mrs. Scott is glad.

6. **The Polite 'You'. Vd.** is short for **usted** which, in turn, is short for **Vuestra Merced**—Your Mercy. Similarly, the plural, **Vds.—ustedes—Vuestras Mercedes**—Your Mercies. **Vd.** and **Vds.** with the 3rd person singular and plural of the verb, are used except when addressing children, relatives, close friends and colleagues of similar standing.

7. **Punctuation.** Spanish punctuation differs in some respects from English. Note the use of dashes instead of inverted commas in direct speech and the position of the quotation marks. Note also the inverted exclamation mark at the beginning of the exclamation. You will later meet an inverted question mark as well.

EJERCICIOS

1. Pronounce the following nouns putting in the correct definite article.

. . . grupo; . . . familia; . . . hotel; . . . conductor;
. . . agencia; . . . profesora; . . . capital; . . . centro;
. . . señor; . . . arquitecto.

2. Put in the correct part of **ser.**
(a) La capital de España . . . Madrid.
(b) El conductor . . . Bill.
(c) Madrid y Toledo . . . interesantes.
(d) Robert dice—Yo . . . el guía.

(e) Bill dice—Robert y yo . . . de la agencia «Sunnidays».
(f) Ella . . . la señora Evans.
(g) El señor Brown . . . arquitecto.
(h) Yo . . . el señor Reilly.
(i) Madrid y Barcelona . . . interesantes.
(j) Vosotros . . . inteligentes.
3. Put in the correct part of **estar**.
   (a) El autocar . . . en Madrid.
   (b) Las cuatro familias . . . contentas.
   (c) Madrid . . . en el centro de España.
   (d) El médico dice—Yo . . . muy contento.
   (e) Y el profesor dice—Sí, . . . contentos.
   (f) Nosotros . . . en el autocar.
   (g) Vosotros . . . en Francia.
   (h) Las cuatro familias . . . en el hotel.
   (i) Tú . . . contento en el Hotel Santo Domingo.
   (j) El estudiante . . . contento.
4. Choose between the two words for is (es *and* está).
   (a) Bilbao . . . en el norte de España.
   (b) El hotel . . . elegante.
   (c) El señor Brown . . . inteligente.
   (d) Robert . . . contento.
   (e) Bill . . . inglés.
   (f) El hotel . . . en el centro.
   (g) Robert . . . el guía.
   (h) La excursión . . . interesante.
   (i) Bill . . . en el autocar.
   (j) El señor Reilly . . . dentista.
5. Put in the correct part of **ser** or **estar**.
   (a) El arquitecto y el dentista . . . inteligentes.
   (b) El grupo inglés . . . en la capital.
   (c) Madrid . . . la capital.
   (d) El señor Reilly dice—Yo . . . contento en la capital.
   (e) El señor Scott dice—Yo . . . médico.
   (f) El señor Brown dice—Yo . . . en España.
   (g) —Sí—dice la señora Brown—tú . . . en España.
   (h) Nosotros . . . contentos en España.
   (i) Ellas . . . profesoras.
   (j) El . . . futbolista magnífico.

6. Give the meanings of the following:
   soy; sois; estás; Vd. es; ella está; estoy; Vds. están; estáis; somos; eres.
7. Say or write the following numbers as Spanish words:
   6; 1; 9; 4; 3; 7; 10; 2; 5; 8.

LECCION 2

EL HOTEL ES BUENO

El Hotel Santo Domingo es **grande,** elegante y moderno.
Las habitaciones son **cómodas** y modernas.
La recepcionista dice—**Aquí** están las listas de las habitaciones:

Habitación número

once (11)	los señores Brown
doce (12)	los señores Reilly
trece (13)	el doctor y la señora Scott
catorce (14)	los señores Evans
quince (15)	John y Janet Brown
dieciséis (16)	Patrick y Michael Reilly
diecisiete (17)	Duncan y Morag Scott
dieciocho (18)	Olwen y Bronwen Evans
diecinueve (19)	las señoritas Chester, Lancaster, Stafford y York
veinte (20)	Peter Field y Philip Ball.

Peter Field y Philip Ball son los dos futbolistas. Las señoritas
Chester, Lancaster, Stafford y York son las cuatro profesoras.
El conserje tiene **las llaves** de las habitaciones números
once a veinte. Los diez matrimonios y los seis estudiantes
están en **otro piso. Las maletas** están en el **ascensor.**
Todas las habitaciones son bonitas. Son **muy** grandes con
cuartos de baño modernos.
—Tenemos un baño **amarillo**—dice Janet.
—Tenemos **una alfombra** amarilla y dos **camas pequeñas**
—dice Morag—y hay persianas en **las ventanas.**
—Y yo tengo una alfombra **roja** en **el suelo** y un balcón
con dos **sillas** y **una mesa** pequeña.
Las habitaciones están **arriba.** Y **abajo** están **la cocina,**
el comedor, la sala, el bar y hay una terraza bonita. En la
terraza hay sillas y mesas rojas.

Todo el grupo tiene hambre. **La cena** es muy **buena.** El
doctor Scott dice—Yo tengo sed.
—Aquí está el vino. Es muy bueno—dice el señor Evans.
Todos están **cansados pero** están satisfechos, porque el
hotel es bueno y mañana hay una excursión a unas partes
interesantes de la capital.

VOCABULARIO

abajo	downstairs
la alfombra	the carpet
amarillo	yellow
aquí	here
arriba	upstairs
el ascensor	the lift
bonito	pretty, nice
bueno	good
la cama	the bed
cansado	tired
la cena	supper
la cocina	the kitchen
el comedor	the dining room
cómodo	comfortable
con	with
el cuarto de baño	the bathroom
grande	big
la habitación	the room, bedroom
la llave	the key
la maleta	the suitcase
la mesa	the table
muy	very
otro	other, another
pequeño	small
pero	but
el piso	the storey
rojo	red
la silla	the chair
el suelo	the floor
la ventana	the window

GRAMATICA

8. **Plural of the Definite Article.** The masculine plural form of *the* is **los** and the feminine plural is **las.**

Examples:

| los baños | the baths | las maletas | the suitcases |
| los ascensores | the lifts | las llaves | the keys |

Note:
The definite article, singular or plural must be put in before a noun in its generic sense, e.g. Las capitales son interesantes.

9. **Plural of Nouns and Adjectives.** Those ending in a vowel add **s** to form the plural while those ending in a consonant add **es.**

Examples:
pisos   storeys;   cocinas   kitchens
hoteles elegantes   smart hotels.

Note:
habitación, habitaciones; excursión, excursiones.
The accent is dropped in the plural because the stress automatically falls on the next to last syllable.

10. **The Indefinite Article** *a* (*an*) is translated by **un** (masculine) and **una** (feminine). The plural forms, **unos** and **unas** mean *some* or *a few.*

Examples:

un matrimonio	a married couple;
unos matrimonios	some (a few) married couples
una alfombra	a carpet;
unas alfombras	some (a few) carpets.

Note:
unos and **unas,** meaning SOME, are frequently omitted, particularly after the verb **tener,** to have.

Examples:
Tenemos sillas cómodas. We have SOME comfortable chairs.

11. **Position and Agreement of Adjectives.** Adjectives may be placed either before or after the noun; bonitas alfombras, vino bueno.

When the adjective comes first it supposes more attention to it; while placing the adjective after the noun emphasises the noun rather than the adjective. At this stage the student will find fewer pitfalls in putting the adjective after the noun; **ventanas grandes, comedores modernos.**

Exceptions to notice are numbers and other adjectives implying quantities and amounts which are always placed BEFORE the noun; **tres camas,** *three beds;* **mucho vino,** *much wine.*

All adjectives must agree in number (singular or plural) and gender (masculine or feminine) with the nouns they describe.

Examples:

un bar moderno; una terraza bonita; unos grupos grandes; unas mesas rojas.

(Remember that those adjectives which do not end in o remain the same in the singular for both genders.)

When two adjectives describe the same noun and both come after it, they are linked by y—and.

Examples:

unas sillas cómodas y rojas   some comfortable red chairs

One adjective may describe more than one noun:

(a) If it goes before, it agrees with the first noun; cómodas salas y comedores.

(b) If it is placed afterwards, it agrees with them in the plural; la alfombra y la silla amarillas. If any one of the nouns is masculine, the adjective will be masculine; cocinas, terrazas y bares modernos.

12. The verb **tener** to have:

(yo) tengo	I have
(tú) tienes	you have (familiar, singular)
(él)	
(ella) tiene	he, she, it has
(Vd.)	you have (polite, singular)
(nosotros) tenemos	we have

(vosotros) tenéis   you have (familiar, plural)
(ellos)
(ellas) tienen   they have
(Vds.)   you have (polite, plural)
Learn by heart: Tener
                 tengo
                 tienes
                 tiene
                 tenemos
                 tenéis
                 tienen

13. **Expressions with tener:**
Spanish frequently uses **tener** *to have* where English
uses *to be* in such expressions as:
tener hambre—to be hungry
   (tengo hambre—I am hungry)
tener sed—to be thirsty
   (tengo sed—I am thirsty)

14. **Hay.** The impersonal verb **hay** means *there is, there are.*

15. **Todo and todos.** As a noun **todo** means *all, everything*
while **todos** means *everybody, everyone.*
The adjective is tod**o**, tod**a**, tod**os**, tod**as**.
Examples:
   todo el vino—all the wine
   toda la familia—all the family
   todos los conductores—all the drivers
   todas las habitaciones—all the rooms

EJERCICIOS

1. Pronounce the following words, putting in the correct form
of the definite article.
. . . habitación; . . . piso; . . . ascensor; . . . sillas;
. . . conserje; . . . cuarto de baño; . . . mesa;
. . . excursiones; . . . ventana; . . . persianas.

2. Pronounce the following words, putting in the correct form
of the indefinite article.
. . . lista; . . . estudiante; . . . camas; . . . bar;
. . . terrazas; . . . comedores; . . . cocina; . . . maleta;
. . . vino; . . . cena.

3. Make the adjective in brackets agree with the noun:
   (a) la alfombra (rojo)   (f) un hotel (bonito)
   (b) el ascensor (grande)   (g) unas ventanas (grande)
   (c) la habitación (pequeño)   (h) una cama (cómodo)
   (d) las cenas (bueno)   (i) excursiones (interesante)
   (e) los comedores (elegante)   (j) unos señores (cansado)

4. Write in Spanish, paying attention to both position and agreement of adjectives:
   (a) the big hotel   (f) some red chairs
   (b) the yellow bath   (g) the good footballer
   (c) a good supper   (h) a few modern tables
   (d) small windows   (i) the six students
   (e) a pretty terrace   (j) a tired driver

5. Put in the correct part of **tener.**
   (a) Janet . . . una cama pequeña.
   (b) El doctor Scott . . . vino.
   (c) Yo . . . una habitación bonita.
   (d) Todos . . . habitaciones cómodas.
   (e) Las profesoras . . . hambre.
   (f) La recepcionista . . . las listas.
   (g) Nosotros . . . sed.
   (h) El estudiante . . . una silla muy cómoda.
   (i) Las habitaciones . . . balcones.
   (j) Estoy cansado y . . . sed.

6. Translate into English:
   Todos están cansados. Tienen hambre y sed pero están contentos en el Hotel Santo Domingo en el centro de Madrid, porque todo es muy bueno aquí. Hay habitaciones grandes y cómodas y abajo hay muchos cuartos modernos. Mañana—dice Robert—hay una excursión muy interesante.

7. Write the following sentences in Spanish, choosing carefully between **ser** and **estar.**
   (a) The driver is English.
   (b) The guide is in the hotel.
   (c) They are tired.
   (d) The room is comfortable.
   (e) The windows are big.
   (f) The chairs are on the balcony.
   (g) We are satisfied because the hotel is good.

(h) Madrid is in Spain.

(i) I am small.

(j) You (polite, singular) are a dentist.

8. Write the following numbers as Spanish words:

11; 14; 16; 17; 19; 2; 5; 10; 12; 13; 15; 18; 20; 6; 7.

LECCION 3

MADRID DE DIA

Hoy es **domingo**, el día de la **primera** excursión: Madrid de día. Robert está con el grupo pero Bill está cansado y no **pasea** con los turistas. Está todo el día en la cama porque **tiene mucho sueño.** Los otros pasean por la capital y visitan varios **sitios** interesantes.

Las cuatro profesoras **miran** todos los monumentos con interés.

—¿Dónde estamos **ahora?**—**pregunta** la señorita York.

—Estamos en la Plaza de España. Aquí estála estatua de don Quijote y Sancho Panza—**contesta** Robert. —La estatua es muy famosa.

— ¿Cuáles son **los edificios** grandes de la Plaza de España?

—Son los dos **rascacielos** de Madrid, el Edificio de España y la Torre de Madrid.

Miran el Palacio **Real** pero no entran. **Llegan** a la Plaza Mayor, centro **antiguo** de Madrid.

—Es **precioso**—dicen todos.

De la Plaza Mayor pasean a la Puerta del Sol, otra parte muy **vieja**, donde hay mucha **circulación.** Aquí entran en el Metro y **viajan** a la estación de Banco.

— ¿Dónde estamos ahora?—pregunta la señorita Chester.

— ¿Cuál es el edificio grande?

— ¿Y qué es el arco antiguo?—pregunta la señorita Stafford.

Otra profesora pregunta— ¿Cuál es **la fuente** en el centro de la plaza?

Robert contesta—Ahora estamos en la Avenida de José Antonio. Es muy famosa. Miramos **la Calle** de Alcalá. **También** es famosa. La puerta antigua es la Puerta de Alcalá, el edificio grande es el Palacio de Comunicaciones y la fuente es la de Cibeles. ¿No es bonita?

—Sí, es preciosa—dice la señorita Stafford. —Todo es muy bonito, la parte antigua y los sitios **nuevos** también. Y ahora miro **los escaparates** de la Avenida de José Antonio.

14

SPANISH ONCE A WEEK

—Yo entro en un café—dice Robert. —Hay muchos cafés buenos en la Gran Vía y tengo mucha sed. —Yo también—dice la señorita Lancaster. —Entro en un café también. No entramos en **las tiendas** hoy porque es domingo. Todos entran en el Café California porque tienen sed.

VOCABULARIO

A.

ahora	now
antiguo	old, ancient
la calle	the street
la circulación	movement of people and traffic
contestar	to answer
el edificio	the building
el escaparate	the shop window
la fuente	the fountain
hoy	today
llegar (a)	the arrive (at)
mirar	to look at
nuevo	new
pasear	to take a walk, to stroll, to promenade
por	through
precioso	beautiful, exquisite
primero	first
el rascacielos	sky-scraper
real	royal
sitio	place
también	also
la tienda	the shop
viajar	to travel
viejo, (antiguo —less deprecating)	old

B. Los días de la semana—*the days of the week*.
Note that capital letters are not used.

lunes—Monday	miércoles—Wednesday
martes—Tuesday	jueves—Thursday

viernes—Friday   domingo—Sunday
sábado—Saturday

All days are masculine, e.g. el lunes—(the) Monday.
Note also el lunes—on Monday, los lunes—on Mondays.

C. ¿Qué?—*what?* ¿cuál?—*what?* and ¿dónde?—*where?* require an accent when used as question words. This applies
to all question words.

D. ¿Qué? translates *what?* when a description or definition is
required.

¿Cuál? translates *what?* before the verb *to be* when no
description or definition is required.

Examples:
¿Qué es un autocar?
¿Cuál es la calle?

E. Tener sueño—to be sleepy. Notice the use of mucho
(not muy) in expressions with tener, e.g. tiene mucho
sueño—he is *very* sleepy, tengo mucha sed—I am *very*
thirsty.

GRAMATICA

16. **Present Tense of Regular Verbs,** 1st conjugation,
ending in -ar:

Mirar *to look at*

(yo)	miro	I look at, I am looking at
(tú)	miras	you look at, you are looking at
(él)	mira	he looks at, he is looking at
(ella)	mira	she looks at, she is looking at
(Vd.)	mira	you look at, you are looking at
(nosotros)	miramos	we look at, we are looking at
(vosotros)	miráis	you look at, you are looking at
(ellos)	miran	they look at, they are looking at
(ellas)	miran	they look at, they are looking at
(Vds.)	miran	you look at, you are looking at

Learn by heart: miro
miras
mira
miramos
miráis
miran

The two forms of the present tense in English, *I enter, I am entering*, are expressed by the one form in Spanish, **entro**.

17. **Negative and Interrogative:**
    (a) **The Negative.** A statement or question is made negative by inserting **no** before the verb.

Examples:
Bill tiene sueño. Bill is sleepy.
Bill **no** tiene sueño. Bill is *not* sleepy.
Robert entra en un café. Robert enters a café.
Robert **no** entra en un café. Robert *does not* enter a café.

   (b) **The Interrogative.** If the subject is stated, a question is formed by inverting the subject and verb.

Examples:
Statement: Bill es el conductor. Bill is the driver.
Question: ¿Es Bill el conductor? Is Bill the driver?
Statement: Yo tengo hambre. I am hungry.
Question: ¿Tengo yo hambre? Am I hungry?
Notice the position of the adjective in a question.
¿Es viejo el edificio? Is the building old?
¿Son nuevas las tiendas? Are the shops new?

   (c) **The Negative-Interrogative.** In a negative question the Spanish **no** remains in front of the verb.

Example:
¿No es dentista? Is he *not* a dentist?
¿No tienen maletas? Have*n't* they (any) suitcases?
Finally, when an answer begins with *yes* or *no* the comma and the pause are important.

Examples:
No, es arquitecto. No, he is an architect.
No es arquitecto. He is not an architect.
No, no es arquitecto. No, he is not an architect.

EJERCICIOS

1. Put in the correct part of the verb in brackets.
   (a) Los turistas (pasear) en la capital.
   (b) Yo (entrar) en un café.

(c) —¿Dónde (estar) las tiendas?—(preguntar) la señora.

(d) El guía (contestar).

(e) Nosotros (viajar) en autocar.

(f) Tú (llegar) a la tienda.

(g) Vosotros (miran) el palacio.

(h) Vd. (entrar) en el ascensor.

(i) Vds. (ser) muy buenos.

(j) El médico (llegar) el jueves.

2. Make the statements negative.

(a) Vd. mira los escaparates.

(b) Las fuentes son bonitas.

(c) Estamos en un edificio grande.

(d) ¿Viajan en el Metro?

(e) Llego a la capital.

3. Change the statements into questions.

(a) Soy profesor.

(b) Peter y Philip son dos futbolistas.

(c) Tenemos vino.

(d) Miro el palacio grande.

(e) La estatua es muy famosa.

4. Answer the questions in Spanish.

(a) ¿Dónde está la Plaza de España?

(b) ¿Qué es el edificio grande?

(c) ¿Dónde están los dos rascacielos de Madrid?

(d) ¿Qué es la señorita Lancaster?

(e) ¿Qué son Peter y Philip?

5. Give the opposites of:

viejo; antiguo; grande; preguntar; no.

6. Translate into Spanish:

On Sunday the tourists stroll in the famous avenue. They arrive at the square and look at the statue and the sky-scrapers. They also look at a fountain in another square.

"Everything is exquisite," says one of the ladies.

"Yes, everything is very nice," answers one of the gentlemen, "but now I am hungry and thirsty."

The lady and gentleman and all the other tourists enter a café with the guide.

LECCION 4

POR LA MAÑANA

Hace mucho calor en Madrid. Todos tienen sed. La familia Scott está en un café.

—¿Qué **bebéis?**—pregunta el doctor Scott.

—Bebo un café—dice la señora.

—Bebo una limonada—dice Morag.

—¿**Coméis algo?**

—Sí, como **un pastel**—responde Morag.

Duncan **toma** fruta **solamente.**

Por la mañana no hay excursión. El grupo tiene la mañana **libre.** Las profesoras preguntan— ¿Dónde hay un parque?

—Hay muchos parques en Madrid—contesta Robert. —El parque del Retiro es muy bonito.

—Bueno, paseamos por el parque del Retiro—dicen las señoritas.

—**Querida**—dice el doctor Scott— ¿dónde hay un banco?

— ¿**Por qué?**—pregunta la señora Scott.

Porque no tengo dinero—responde el médico. —Tengo que **cambiar dinero** por la mañana porque **por la tarde** hacemos una excursión a Toledo.

—Bueno—dice la señora—visito **la peluquería. —Hasta la vista.**

—**Adiós, hasta luego.**

El doctor Scott entra en el banco. Cambia diez **libras.** La señora Scott entra en una peluquería de las en la Gran Vía. Es un salón muy elegante. La señora Scott comprende el español **bastante** bien y habla un **poco** también.

La peluquera dice—Buenos días, señora. ¿Cómo está Vd.?

—Muy **bien,** gracias. ¿Y Vd?—dice la señora Scott.

—Muy bien. ¿**Lavar y marcar?**

—Sí, lavar y marcar, **por favor.**

— ¿Necesita Vd. también una manicura?

—Sí, necesito una manicura.

El doctor Scott **espera** a la señora en el hotel.

—Querida, estás muy elegante—dice.

—Y tú estás **rico** ¿verdad?—pregunta **la mujer.**

—Bastante.

—Bueno, en la Gran Vía hay una tienda donde **venden** sombreros preciosos. Hay un sombrero estupendo. Es amarillo y muy grande y tiene. . . .

— ¿**Cuánto** es?

—Solamente diez libras.

—¡Caramba! Soy hombre **pobre de nuevo.**

VOCABULARIO

A.

algo	something
bastante	quite
beber	to drink
bien	well
cambiar	to change
comer	to eat
de nuevo	again
el dinero	money
esperar	to wait (for)
hablar	to speak
lavar y marcar	shampoo and set
la libra	the pound
libre	free
la mujer	the wife, woman
el pastel	the cake
la peluquera	the hairdresser
la peluquería	the hairdresser's shop
pobre	poor
poco	little, few
por favor	please
querida	dear, darling
rico	rich
solamente	only
tomar	to take, have (food and drink)
vender	to sell

B. Greetings and Farewells:

Buenos días	Good day, morning
Buenas tardes	Good afternoon, evening
Buenas noches	Good night

Note:

Por la mañana	In the morning
Por la tarde	In the afternoon, evening
De noche, de día	At night, in the daytime.
¿Cómo está Vd?	How do you do?
Muy bien, gracias	Very well, thank you

a more colloquial enquiry is:

¿Qué tal?	How are you?
Adiós	Goodbye
Hasta la vista	Goodbye for the present, au revoir
Hasta luego	Goodbye, till later

C. Question Words:

(a) ¿Por qué? *Why?*

Examples:

¿Por qué bebe Vd. café Porque tengo sed.
Why are you drinking coffee? Because I am thirsty.

Note:

Be careful to distinguish between ¿por qué? meaning *why* and porque meaning *because.*

(b) ¿Cuánto? (a, -os, as)? *how much, how many?*

Examples:

¿Cuánto dinero tiene Vd? *How much* money have you?
¿Cuántas habitaciones hay en el hotel? *How many* rooms are there in the hotel?

(c) ¿Verdad? Rhetorical question meaning isn't it, aren't you, won't you? etc.

GRAMATICA

18. **Present Tense of Regular Verbs, 2nd conjugation, ending in -er:**

Comer *to eat*

como   I eat, I am eating
comes

come
comemos
coméis
comen

19. **Irregular verb, Hacer** *to do, to make:*
In the present indicative this verb is irregular only in the first person singular. It is an important verb as it is the basis for many idiomatic phrases.

hago
haces
hace
hacemos
hacéis
hacen

Hacer is used in expressions relating to the weather.

Examples:

Hace mucho calor.   It is very hot.
Hace buen día.   It is a fine day.

but **Tener** is used for persons:

Tengo calor.   I am hot.

20. **Personal 'a':**
The personal 'a' is used before a direct object of a verb, except TENER, when the object is a noun indicating a definite or particular person, personified thing, well-loved place or pet.

Examples:

El médico visita a la mujer.
Visito a Madrid.

EJERCICIOS

1. Answer the questions in Spanish:
   (a) ¿Dónde está la familia Scott?
   (b) ¿Qué bebe la señora Scott?
   (c) ¿Qué toma Duncan?
   (d) ¿Hay una excursión por la mañana?
   (e) ¿Hay un parque bonito en Madrid?
   (f) ¿Habla español la señora Scott?

(g) ¿Por qué visita el doctor un banco?

(h) ¿Qué hace el doctor en el banco?

(i) ¿Dónde está la peluquería?

(j) ¿Dónde espera el doctor a la señora?

2. Insert the personal 'a' into the sentences that require it:

(a) Los turistas esperan   Robert.

(b) El guía contesta   las profesoras.

(c) —Sí—dice Robert   los futbolistas.

(d) La señora mira   los escaparates.

(e) El señor Evans tiene   mujer elegante.

3. Insert the correct form of the verb in brackets:

(a) Las estatuas famosas de don Quijote y Sancho Panza (estar) en la Plaza de España.

(b) Yo (mirar) los escaparates.

(c) La señorita Chester (ser) profesora.

(d) El guía (tener) mucho sueño.

(e) Nosotros (comer) mucha fruta.

(f) Tú (comprender) el español muy bien.

(g) Las señoritas (tener) calor.

(h) Vosotros (pasear) en el parque.

(i) Yo (tener) un sombrero precioso.

(j) Los futbolistas (esperar) a Robert.

4. Insert the correct form of the verb HACER.

(a) Yo   una excursión por la mañana.

(b) Tú   la cama.

(c) En Madrid   buen tiempo.

(d) ¿Qué   Vd?

(e) Nosotros   las maletas.

5. Translate:

Doctor Scott strolls in the park. Mrs. Scott visits the hairdresser's. In the afternoon they have coffee at the hotel. They talk with the guide. He asks, "Are you satisfied at the Hotel Santo Domingo?" They answer, "Yes, we are satisfied. The hotel is very comfortable."

6. Put the following sentences into the plural:

(a) El futbolista come un pastel.

(b) El conductor tiene mucho sueño.

(c) El estudiante toma café.

(d) Hago la maleta.

3

(e) Está aquí el martes.
(f) La silla es muy cómoda.
(g) La habitación es moderna.
(h) Tengo una maleta nueva.
(i) El hombre es arquitecto.
(j) La mesa roja está en el balcón.

7. For each of the sentences begun in section A choose the appropriate ending from section B.

A	B
(a) El autocar está	pequeñas.
(b) Las mesas son	moderno.
(c) Los estudiantes toman	cinco.
(d) —Buenos días	médico.
(e) El señor Mateos es	cansado.
(f) —Adiós—dice	quince.
(g) El hotel es	en la plaza.
(h) Dos y tres son	café.
(i) Seis y nueve son	Señor Pérez.
(j) El señor Gómez está	el señor García.

LECCION 5

PATRICK APRENDE ALGO

El conductor y el guía están en el autocar. Esperan a los turistas. Pronto llegan los Reilly. **Abren la puerta** del autocar y **suben.** Pocos minutos **después** llegan los otros; los estudiantes, las profesoras, las otras familias, los matrimonios y un futbolista. **¿Adónde** van? Van a Toledo, **una antigua ciudad** a sesenta y nueve (69) kilómetros de Madrid. Robert mira a los turistas. —Hay solamente treinta y siete (37)—dice. — ¿**Quién** no está? El futbolista contesta —Mi **amigo** no está pero llega ahora. El otro futbolista abre la puerta y sube. —Perdón—dice. —Gracias. Todos están contentos y hablan mucho. Solamente Patrick no habla. Escribe **una postal.** —Patrick ¿qué haces?—pregunta John. —Escribo a uno de mis amigos irlandeses. Espera **recibir** una postal con una vista de Madrid.

Antes de llegar los turistas a Toledo, Robert dice —En Toledo vamos a visitar el Alcázar, **la casa** de El Greco, la **iglesia** de Santo Tomé y la Catedral.

Bajan del autocar en una plaza pequeña. Robert y los turistas van al Alcázar, un edificio espléndido y muy famoso, pero Bill no va. Tiene que **cuidar del** autocar. El grupo inglés va después a la casa de El Greco.

— ¿Quién es El Greco?—pregunta Patrick.

— ¿Qué **aprendes** en tu colegio, Patrick?—pregunta el señor Reilly. —El pintor El Greco no **vive** ahora, pero es famoso y unas de sus **obras** están aquí en Toledo. En la Iglesia de Santo Tomé hay una obra famosa «**El entierro** del Conde de Orgaz» y hay también en Toledo una de San Bernardo y otra de San Pedro. Otras obras están en el Museo del Prado en Madrid adonde vamos mañana.

—El profesor en nuestro colegio habla solamente del arte moderno—dice Patrick.

Toledo no es moderno. Sus calles son antiguas y sus casas son pequeñas. Solamente la catedral es grande. **Enfrente de** la ciudad hay una vista magnífica de **la meseta** central y **el río** Tajo.

—Bueno—dicen todos. —Las excursiones son muy interesantes.

—Sí—dice el dentista, —son interesantes y Patrick aprende algo.

VOCABULARIO

A.

abrir	to open
el alcázar	the fortress
el amigo	the friend
antes (de)	before
aprender	to learn
bajar	to get down, get off
la casa	the house
la ciudad	the city, large town
cuidar (de)	to take care (of), look after
después	afterwards
después de	after
enfrente (de)	opposite (to)
el entierro	the burial
la iglesia	the church
la meseta	the plateau
la obra	the work, masterpiece
el pintor	the painter
la postal	the postcard
la puerta	the door
recibir	to receive
el río	the river
subir	to get onto
vivir	to live

B. More Question Words:

¿adónde?	where to?
¿quién, quiénes?	who?

C. Numerals:

21	veintiuno	30	treinta
22	veintidós	31	treinta y uno
23	veintitrés	42	cuarenta y dos
24	veinticuatro	53	cincuenta y tres
25	veinticinco	64	sesenta y cuatro
26	veintiséis	75	setenta y cinco
27	veintisiete	86	ochenta y seis
28	veintiocho	97	noventa y siete
29	veintinueve		

Note:

Tengo veintiuno

but Tengo veintiún postales. I have twenty postcards and one postcard.

D. The Names of Saints:

The masculine form **Santo** is shortened to **San** except before names beginning with T or D. The feminine form is always **Santa**.

GRAMATICA

21. **Present Tense Regular Verbs, 3rd conjugation, ending in -ir:**

These have the same endings as the -er verbs except for the 1st and 2nd persons plural.

Escribir   *to write*

escribo   I write, I am writing
escribes
escribe
escribimos
escribís
escriben

22. **Irregular Verb, Ir**   *to go*

This is a completely irregular verb and must be learned by heart from the start.

voy   I go, I am going
vas
va

> vamos
> vais
> van

Ir a.

This means *to be going to* and is followed by an infinitive.

Examples:
Voy a comer algo. I am going to eat something.
Van a escribir una postal. They are going to write a postcard.

23. **The Infinitive:**
The verb which follows another verb or a preposition is an infinitive.

Examples:

Esperan entrar en la iglesia.	They are waiting to enter the church.
Tenemos que bajar aquí.	We have to get off here.
Antes de visitar la iglesia visitamos la catedral.	Before visiting the church we visit the cathedral.

Notice that the Spanish infinitive often replaces the English present participle.

24. **Possessive Adjectives:**
These agree in number and gender with the noun possessed.

mi	my
tu	your
su	his, her, its, your (polite)
nuestro	our
vuestro	your
su	their, your (polite)

If there is any doubt as to whom **su** refers, the forms **de él, de ella, de Vd, de ellos, de ellas, de Vds.** may be added.

Examples:
El profesor y sus estudiantes van a su casa de él.
The teacher and his students go to *his* house.

25. **Al and del:**
A el becomes **al**, *to the, at the* and de el becomes **del**, *of the, from the*, except when **El** begins with a capital letter.

Examples:
La casa de El Greco.
Va a El Perú.

EJERCICIOS

1. Answer the questions:
   (a) ¿Dónde está la casa de El Greco?
   (b) ¿Adónde van los turistas?
   (c) ¿Quién es Robert?
   (d) ¿Por qué no habla Patrick?
   (e) ¿Cuántos turistas hay en el grupo?
2. Make up sentences beginning with the question words:
   (a) ¿Qué . . .? (b) ¿Cuántas . . .? (c) ¿Quién . . .?
   (d) ¿Adónde . . .? (e) ¿Quiénes . . .?
3. Put in the missing words:
   (a) Llegamos antes . . . los otros.
   (b) El martes vamos . . . museo.
   (c) Es la iglesia de . . . José.
   (d) Despúes de entrar . . . la habitación, abrimos las ventanas.
   (e) Quince y veintiuno son . . .
4. Put in the possessive adjectives:
   (a) Patrick dice que . . . amigo vive en Irlanda.
   (b) No aprendemos el español en . . . colegio.
   (c) Estoy en . . . habitación.
   (d) Los turistas miran . . . habitaciones.
   (e) Patrick y Michael, ¿dónde están . . . maletas?
5. Put in the correct form of the verb in brackets:
   (a) El guía (abrir) la puerta.
   (b) Los estudiantes no (aprender) el español.
   (c) Tengo que (ir) al dentista.
   (d) Nosotros (bajar) aquí.
   (e) ¿Dónde (vivir) vosotros?
   (f) Van a (llegar) por la tarde.
   (g) ¿Adónde (ir) Vd?
   (h) ¿Quiénes (ser) el guía y el conductor?
   (i) (Hacer) mucho calor en Madrid.
   (j) El furbolista (subir) al autocar.

6. Translate into English:

El lunes por la tarde los turistas van a Toledo. Hacen la excursión en su autocar cómodo y llegan pronto a la interesante y antigua ciudad. Hace mucho calor en las calles pero no hace calor en los edificios que entran; el alcázar, la iglesia, la catedral y la casa del pintor greco. Los turistas miran todo con interés y después hablan mucho de su excursión. Escriben a sus amigos que esperan recibir postales.

LECCION 6

UN NIÑO PEREZOSO

Es martes, el día 23 de **junio**. Hace mucho calor en la ciudad. Por la mañana la familia Brown va a **una piscina**. **Los niños nadan** con **el padre**, y **la madre toma el sol**. **Lee una revista** y después escribe unas postales a **los parientes** de Inglaterra.

—Janet—pregunta a **la hija**— ¿a cuántos estamos?

—No sé, mamá.

La niña pregunta a su **hermano** —John, ¿sabes qué fecha es? —Sí, estamos a 23 de junio.

Cuando la familia toma café, la madre dice —Niños, tenéis que escribir unas postales a **los primos**. Yo escribo a los abuelos, **al tío** de Londres y **las tías** de Edimburgo.

— ¿A quién escribe papá?—pregunta John.

—A los tíos de Manchester—responde el padre.

Después de tomar los **bocadillos** y el café, la madre dice —Niños, aquí está **la ropa**.

—Pero no **tenemos frío**.

—No, no **hace frío** aquí en Madrid pero pronto vamos a la calle.

— ¿Adónde vamos?

—Vamos a **un estanco** porque tenemos que **comprar sellos** y **echar** las postales.

—Papá, ¿qué es un estanco?

—Es una tienda pequeña donde venden solamente sellos, cigarrillos, otras clases de tabaco y cerillas.

—**Las cajitas de cerillas** son muy bonitas—dice Janet.

—Hay **cuadros** pequeños en ellas. Una amiga del colegio es coleccionista de esas cajitas.

—**Entonces** tenemos que comprar unas. Pero esta tarde vas a ver cuadros preciosos en el Museo del Prado.

— ¿Es el museo aquel edificio grande en el Paseo del Prado?

—Sí.

— ¿Tenemos que **pasar mucho tiempo** allí?

—No, no mucho. Después vamos al Parque del Retiro.
¿Escribes esa postal a los primos antes de salir de aquí?
—Sí, porque después de hacer eso, no voy a **trabajar más**
durante mis vacaciones.
—**Hijo**, eres un niño muy **perezoso**.

VOCABULARIO

A.

allí	there
el bocadillo	the sandwich
la cajita de cerillas	the box of matches
comprar	to buy
el cuadro	the picture
cuando	when
echar	to post
entonces	then
el estanco	the state controlled shop
leer	to read
más	more
nadar	to swim
perezoso	lazy
la piscina	the swimming pool
la revista	the magazine
la ropa	the clothes
el sello	the stamp
trabajar	to work

B. La Familia:

el abuelo, grandfather; la abuela, grandmother; los
abuelos, grandparents

el hermano, brother; la hermana, sister; los hermanos,
brothers (and sisters)

el hijo, son; la hija, daughter; los hijos, sons (and daughters)

el niño, boy; la niña, girl; los niños, boys (and girls),
children

el padre, father; la madre, mother; los padres, parents.

el pariente, relation; los parientes, relations

el primo, (male) cousin; la prima (female) cousin; los
primos, cousins

el tío, uncle; la tía, aunt; los tíos, uncles (and aunts)

The definite article is used in preference to the possessive adjective when the meaning is clear.

Example:
Yo vivo con los padres. I live with *my* parents.

C. More Expressions:

hacer frío	to be cold (of weather)
pasar tiempo	to spend time
tener frío	to be cold (of persons)
tomar el sol	to sunbathe

D. Los Meses:

enero	January	julio	July
febrero	February	agosto	August
marzo	March	setiembre	September
abril	April	octubre	October
mayo	May	noviembre	November
junio	June	diciembre	December

E. The Date:
There are two ways of asking the date.
¿Qué es la fecha? What is the date?
¿A cuántos estamos? literally, How many are we at?
Cardinal numbers are used except for the first day of the month.
Es el (día) tres de marzo.
Es el veintinueve de octubre.
but
Es el primero de julio.

GRAMATICA

26. **Three Irregular Verbs:**

Decir *to say, to tell*	**Saber** *to know (facts)*
digo	sé
dices	sabes
dice	sabe
decimos	sabemos
decís	sabéis
dicen	saben

Salir *to leave, to go out*
salgo

sales
sale
salimos
salís
salen

27. Demonstrative Adjectives:

The Spaniards use three forms in contrast to our two:

este, esta, estos, estas	this, these (near the speaker)
ese, esa, esos, esas	that, those (near the listener)
aquel, aquella, aquellos, aquellas	that, those (over there, near neither speaker nor listener)

28. Demonstrative Pronouns:

These are identical to the demonstrative adjectives except that they bear an accent on the stressed syllable.

éste, ésta, éstos, éstas	this one, these ones
ése, ésa, ésos, ésas	that one, those ones
aquél, aquélla, aquéllos, aquéllas	that one, those ones (over there)

Note:

The neuter forms are used when the gender is uncertain. They do not have accents. One form expresses both singular and plural.

esto.

eso.

aquel.

Example:

¿Qué es eso?	What is that?

29. Diminutives. The endings *ito* and *illo*.

Examples:

la caja	the box,	la cajita	the little box
el niño	the child,	el niñito	the small child
la casa	the house,	la casita	the cottage
la ventana	the window,	la ventanilla	the small window, especially of vehicles

The endings can also be used as endearments.

abuelita	granny dear.

EJERCICIOS

1. Put in the correct form of the irregular verbs in brackets.
   (a) Philip (decir) que su amigo es futbolista estupendo.
   (b) La madre no (salir) por la mañana.
   (c) Los niños no (saber) quien es don Quijote.
   (d) Yo (ir) al parque.
   (e) Tengo hambre después de (estar) en la piscina.
   (f) Yo (hacer) las camas todos los días.
   (g) Niños, (tener) que (salir) pronto.
   (h) Nosotros (decir) que el hotel es bueno.
   (i) John (ser) un niño perezoso.
   (j) Yo no (saber) donde (estar) el museo.
2. Put into Spanish, paying especial attention to the demonstrative adjectives and pronouns:
   (a) There are many rooms; this room is Robert's.
   (b) Is she reading that magazine?
   (c) The money is in that box over there.
   (d) There are many churches; that one is St. Peter's Church.
   (e) What is this?
   (f) I am posting these postcards.
   (g) They live in that street over there.
   (h) We don't know what these are.
   (i) Where is that coach going to?
   (j) This hat is beautiful.
3. Say or write in Spanish:
   (a) It is Thursday, 16th May.
   (b) It is 1st December.
   (c) What date is it?
   (d) The parents are here but the children are in the park.
   (e) Janet's aunt and uncle live in London.
   (f) The windows of the coach do not open.
   (g) The clothes are on the chair.
   (h) The little girl is tired.
   (i) How many days are there is August?
4. Make up sentences using the following expressions:
   (a) tener calor; (b) pasar tiempo; (c) hacer frío; (d) tomar el sol; (e) tener sueño.

5. Expand the following outline:

    Hace calor . . . la piscina . . . bocadillos y café . . . escribir a los parientes . . . comprar sellos.

6. Write out the dates in Spanish words:

    (a) 19th September; (b) 8th April; (c) 12th January; (d) 1st November; (e) 25th July.

LECCION 7

EL MUSEO Y EL PARQUE

— ¿Qué hora es?

—Son las dos y media.

— ¿A qué hora salimos?

—A las cuatro menos cuarto. Es la hora de la siesta. Los estudiantes hablan de la excursión al Prado.

— ¿Vamos en nuestro autocar?

—No. Vamos en el Metro **hasta** la estación de Banco que está **cerca del** museo. Viajar en el Metro es muy **barato**. Robert **saca los billetes** en **la taquilla.** Da un billete a **cada** uno. También tiene que sacar billetes en el museo. **Todo el mundo** sabe que hay cuadros famosos en el Prado pero también hay **joyas,** esculturas etcetera.

Los estudiantes ven las obras de El Greco, Velázquez, Goya, Murillo y Zurbarán. Lo que **creen** de más interés son los cuadros de Goya «El dos de mayo» y «El tres de mayo». Cuando Robert dice que es la hora de ir al Retiro, los estudiantes deciden volver otro día pero los niños dicen que el museo es muy **aburrido. Sin embargo,** en el parque juegan a ser los Infantes de los cuadros de Goya.

Después **juegan** con **una pelota.** Pronto los futbolistas y los estudiantes juegan también. Los otros dan un paseo por este maravilloso parque. Ven el zoo y **el estanque.** Cuando llegan **al lago** los señores deciden tomar **unas barcas** pequeñas pero las señoras deciden tomar té.

El parque es enorme y saben que están **lejos del** Metro. **Mientras** los señores están en el lago, los niños **terminan** de jugar con su pelota. **Corren** hasta el lago y toman unas barcas también. Los padres tienen que esperar mientras los hijos van en las barcas.

A las siete hay mucha **gente** en el Retiro. Es la hora del paseo. Los niños españoles **llevan** la ropa muy bonita y

37

limpia. Los niños ingleses están **sucios** después de correr y
jugar en el suelo.

—¡Qué horror!—dicen las madres.

—No **importa**—contesta Robert. —Son las siete y media,
volvemos al hotel.

VOCABULARIO

aburrido	boring
barato	cheap
la barca	the small boat
el billete	the ticket
cada (uno)	each (one)
cerca (de)	near (to)
correr	to run
creer	to believe
el estanque	the artificial lake
la gente	the people
hasta	until, up to, as far as
importar	to matter
la joya	the jewel
jugar (ue)	to play
el lago	the lake
lejos (de)	far (from)
limpio	clean
llevar	to wear
mientras	while
la pelota	the ball
sacar	to take out
sin embargo	however, nevertheless
sucio	dirty
la taquilla	the ticket office
terminar	to end, finish
todo el mundo	everybody

GRAMATICA

30. **The Time:**

¿Qué hora es? means *what time is it?*

At *one* o'clock the reply is **es la una** but from two o'clock
onwards the verb must be plural.

Examples:

Son las dos	It is two o'clock
Son las tres y cinco	It is five past three
Son las cuatro y diez	It is ten past four
Son las cinco y cuarto	It is quarter past five
Son las seis y veinte	It is twenty past six
Son las siete y veinticinco	It is twenty-five past seven
Son las ocho y media	It is half past eight
Son las nueve menos veinticinco	It is twenty-five to nine
Son las diez menos veinte	It is twenty to ten
Son las once menos cuarto	It is quarter to eleven
Son las doce	It is twelve o'clock

31. **Two more Irregular Verbs:**

Dar *to give*	**Ver** *to see*
doy	veo
das	ves
da	ve
damos	vemos
dais	veis
dan	ven

Note:
dar un paseo—to go for a walk.

32. **Radical Changing Verbs (ue).**
A fairly large proportion of verbs, while taking regular endings, undergo a change of vowel in the stem whenever the stress falls upon it, i.e. throughout the singular and in 3rd person plural. **Volver** and **jugar** belong to the group which change *o* or *u* to *ue*.

Example:

Volver *to return*
vuelvo
vuelves
vuelve
volvemos
volvéis
vuelven

33. Uses of 'que':

(a) As a question word.

¿Qué hace la recepcionista? *What* does the receptionist do?

(b) As a relative pronoun, corresponding to the English *that*, *which* or *who*.

La fruta que compra es barata. The fruit *that* she is buying is cheap.

La revista que lee es aburrida. The magazine *which* he is reading is boring.

La niña que habla inglés está aquí. The girl *who* speaks English is here.

Note:

The relative pronoun "**que**" may never be merely "understood". It must always be stated.

(c) Where in English the inclusion of *that* after a verb is optional, in Spanish **que** MUST be used.

Dicen que las calles están sucias. They say (that) the streets are dirty.

Creo que es verdad. I believe (that) it is true.

(d) As an exclamation que . . .! bears an accent.

¡Qué estupendo!   *How* wonderful!

¡Qué horror!   *How* dreadful!

¡Qué cuadro!   *What* a picture!

¡Qué día más espléndido!   *What* a splendid day!

¡Qué niños más sucios!   *What* dirty children!

(e) **Lo que** translates the pronoun *what*.

Lo que ven es interesante. What they see is interesting.

Tiene lo que necesita. He has what he needs.

EJERCICIOS

1. Give the opposites:
antes; sucio; interesante; grande; cerca; trabajar; los padres; ir a; nuevo; ¡qué horror!
2. Look at the family tree and fill in the blanks in the sentences.

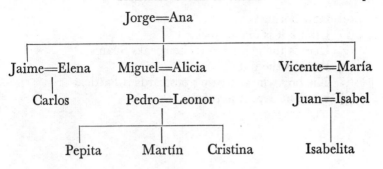

(a) Jorge es el . . . de Miguel.
(b) Miguel es el . . . de Jaime.
(c) María es la . . . de Jaime.
(d) Carlos y Leonor son los . . . de Isabel.
(e) Ana es la . . . de Leonor.
(f) Carlos es . . . . . . de Martín.
(g) Isabelita es . . . . . . de Juan.
(h) Pedro y Leonor son . . . . . . de Cristina.
(i) Vicente y María son . . . . . . de Leonor.
(j) Pepita es . . . . . . de Isabelita.

3. Put in the correct form of the verb:
(a) Los estudiantes (ver) los cuadros.
(b) Nosotros (dar) un paseo en el parque.
(c) El niño (jugar) en la calle.
(d) Yo (ir) a Barcelona.
(e) ¿A qué hora (volver) el profesor?
(f) Nosotros (jugar) cada mañana.
(g) Yo no (saber) que hacen.
(h) Niños, ¿(volver) al colegio?
(i) Niños, ¿dónde (vivir)?
(j) Yo (salir) a las ocho.

4. Write out the times in full.
10.00; 6.30; 8.05; 11.45; 1.00; 4.15; 2.50; 1.25; 8.35; 1.30.

5. Write in Spanish, using **que** in every sentence:
(a) What time is it?
(b) What is he doing?
(c) They say he is a good dentist.
(d) What a pretty park!

(e) How boring!
(f) I think it is one o'clock.
(g) Here is the gentleman who speaks Spanish.
(h) What is the date?
(i) The boy who is writing postcards is Patrick.
(j) What he says is not true.

LECCION 8

VAMOS AL CINE

Mientras cenan dos matrimonios **jóvenes**, los Kelly y los Hilton hablan de los muchos cines y teatros de Madrid.

—¿Quieren Vds. ir a un teatro una noche?—pregunta el señor Hilton.

—Creo que prefiero ir al cine porque no entiendo el español —contesta el señor Kelly. —Mi mujer entiende un poco pero yo no.

—**Estoy de acuerdo**—dice la señora Hilton. —Hay **tantos** cines en Madrid y tantas **películas extranjeras** que siempre hay unas inglesas y americanas. El guía dice que en el "Imperial" **estrenan** "Mil novecientos ochenta y cuatro".

—Pero, ¿no hablan los actores en español?

—No, en esta película hablan inglés.

—¿A qué hora **empiezan las funciones**?

—**A eso de** las siete de la tarde y a las diez y media de la noche. Tenemos que sacar **las entradas con anticipación**. ¿**Cuándo** vamos?

—Vamos mañana, a las diez y media. Esta noche damos un paseo, miramos **los carteles** de los cines en la Gran Vía y sacamos las entradas.

—Si no volvemos hasta la una y media o las dos ¿cómo vamos a entrar en el hotel?—pregunta la señora Kelly. —**Ya sabes** que no hay conserje de noche.

—**El sereno** tiene las llaves de todos **los portales**—contesta su marido. —Tenemos que **dar palmadas** y esperar al sereno. **Es costumbre** dar una propina al sereno.

Y ¿a qué hora **cierran** los portales?

—El sereno empieza trabajar a las once de la noche y termina a las seis y media **de la madrugada**.

—¡Menos mal que no hace frío en Madrid!

—No siempre es **verano**. Dicen que **el clima** de Madrid es:
nueve meses de **invierno**
tres meses de **infierno**.

43

VOCABULARIO

A.

el cartel	the poster
cerrar (ie)	to close
el clima	the climate
la cosa	the thing
la costumbre	the custom
empezar(ie)	to begin
la entrada	the ticket (entertainment)
estrenar	to put on (films and clothes, especially new ones)
extranjero	foreign
la función	the performance, showing
el infierno	Hell
joven	young
la película	the film (cinema)
el portal	the main door
preferir(ie)	to prefer
la propina	the tip
el sereno	the night watchman
tanto, tantos	so much, so many

B. More Question Words:

¿cómo?   how

¿cuándo?   when

C. The Seasons   las estaciones

la primavera	spring	el otoño	autumn
el verano	summer	el invierno	winter

D. Expressions:

a eso de	at about (time)
a eso de las ocho	about 8 o'clock
con anticipación	in advance
dar palmadas	to clap
de la madrugada	in the early morning
estar de acuerdo	to agree
¡menos mal!	it's a good thing
ya sabes	you know very well

GRAMATICA

34. **Radical-changing Verbs (ie).**

The second group are those which change from **e** to **ie** when the stress is on the stem.

Entender   *to understand*
ent**ie**ndo
ent**ie**ndes
ent**ie**nde
entendemos
entendéis
ent**ie**nden

Querer—to want, to love—is an irregular verb but it is regular in the present indicative. It is also radical-changing.

qu**ie**ro
qu**ie**res
qu**ie**re
queremos
queréis
qu**ie**ren

Examples:

¿Cuándo quiere Vd. salir? When do you *want* to leave?
Quiero a los padres. I *love* my parents.

Note:

'Querer' does NOT mean 'to like' except in polite remarks such as:

¿Qué quiere Vd? What would you like?

35. **Language and Nationality:**

(a) **Idiomas.** The names of languages—los idiomas— begin with a small letter and are masculine—el inglés, el español, el francés.

After the verb **hablar,** the definite article is omitted except in the case of **el castellano** (the pure Spanish of Castile).

Examples:

Hablo inglés.	I speak English.
Habla alemán.	He speaks German.
Hablan el castellano.	They speak Spanish.

After all other verbs the definite article must be used.

Examples:

Aprendo el ruso.	I learn Russian.
Leemos el italiano.	We read Italian.
Entienden el portugués.	They understand Portuguese.

(b) **Nacionalidades.** The adjectives of nationality take the same form as the names of the languages but their endings are variable.

Examples:

La niña inglesa vive en Londres. The English girl lives in London.

El restaurante chino está en esta calle. The Chinese restaurant is in this street.

The nouns of nationality are also written with a small letter.

Examples:

un inglés	an Englishman
una inglesa	an Englishwoman
un español	a Spaniard
una española	a Spaniard
un alemán	a German
una alemana	a German

36. **Some Masculine Nouns ending in 'a'.**

El clima and **el idioma** belong to a group of masculine nouns originating from the Greek and retaining the **a** ending.

Further examples:

el día	the day
el mapa	the map
el problema	the problem
el programa	the programme
el telegrama	the telegram

37. **Numbers 100–1,000**

100 ciento	600 seiscientos
200 doscientos	700 **sete**cientos
300 trescientos	800 ochocientos
400 cuatrocientos	900 **nove**cientos
500 **quin**ientos	1,000 mil

All these numbers, when used as adjectives, agree with the nouns they precede.

Examples:

doscientas casas	two hundred houses
quinientos hoteles	five hundred hotels

ciento drops the final **to** before a masculine noun.

Example:

cien edificios	a hundred buildings

Note:

setecientos dos	702
mil novecientos setenta y uno	1971

EJERCICIOS

1. Answer the questions:
   (a) ¿De qué hablan los dos matrimonios jóvenes?
   (b) ¿Por qué prefiere el señor Kelly ir al cine?
   (c) ¿Quién entiende el español?
   (d) ¿Hay muchos cines en Madrid?
   (e) ¿A qué hora empiezan las funciones?
   (f) ¿Cuándo tienen que sacar las entradas?
   (g) ¿Quién abre el portal del hotel de noche?
   (h) ¿Qué da la gente al sereno?
   (i) ¿A qué hora empieza trabajar el sereno?
   (j) ¿Hace calor en Madrid?
2. Conjugate the verbs.
   preferir; jugar; querer; ser; ver.
3. Pair off, in order to form sentences, the phrases in sections A and B.

A	B
La profesora	el francés.
Hablo	hace frío.
Tiene que estudiar	inglesa está aquí.
Viajar en el Metro	trabaja de noche.
El clima de España	el castellano.
En invierno	es la primavera.
El sereno	idiomas.
La primera estación del año	es muy bueno.

Hay cien   no trabaja de noche.
El conserje   es barato.

4. Form sentences using the following expressions:
   a eso de; dar un paseo; estar de acuerdo; sin embargo;
   ya sabes.

5. Translate into Spanish:
   Do you prefer the theatre or the cinema? There are many
   theatres and cinemas in Madrid where they put on films of
   all nationalities, Spanish, English, American, French,
   Italian, etc. You take the tickets in advance. If you return
   to your hotel at about eleven o'clock or afterwards, the
   nightwatchman opens the main door with his key.

6. The initial letters to the answers to the clues spell the name
   of **un hombre que trabaja de noche.**
   (1) Tiene Vd. que comprar uno antes de echar una postal.
   (2) Lo que aprende Vd.
   (3) Los dos edificios grandes en la Plaza de España.
   (4) El pintor de «El entierro del Conde de Orgaz».
   (5) Lo que hace Vd. en la piscina.
   (6) El mes después de setiembre.

LECCION 9

¡QUE MEMORIA TIENE!

El miércoles, el grupo inglés va en autocar a Aranjuez, **un pueblo** situado al borde del **río** Tajo a 45 kilómetros de la capital. Al llegar allí, van en unas barcas hasta el Palacio, donde unos **eligen** entrar **para** mirar los cuadros mientras otros eligen **pasar el rato** al aire libre.
La familia Evans da un paseo por el parque y saca muchas fotografías. **Luego,** el señor Evans saca una foto de su familia **delante del** palacio. Después saca una de las niñas **entre los árboles,** con el río detrás.
Hoy los turistas llevan la merienda. Los Evans comen a la una, porque las niñas dicen que tienen hambre. La madre abre los paquetes y **sirve** la merienda. Hay **pan** con **jamón** y **queso, huevos, naranjas, plátanos** y chocolate. Olwen pide un bocadillo de jamón y Bronwen pide uno de queso. Las niñas beben limonada y los padres toman **cerveza.**
Después de comer el padre **duerme** con **un periódico sobre la cara.** Las niñas sacan una fotografía de su padre. La madre sonríe pero el padre duerme tranquilamente.
—¿Por qué no **dejáis** la máquina y **leéis** un rato?—dice la madre.
—Bueno—contesta Olwen —aquí está mi **libro debajo de** los paquetes.
—No es tuyo, es mío. Tú no tienes el tuyo.
—Si habláis tanto vais a **despertar** a papá.
—Pero mamá, el libro es mío—repite Olwen.
—Si despiertas a papá—repite la madre severamente. . . .
—**Lo siento,** es verdad, mi libro está en el hotel.
Por la tarde los turistas vuelven **lentamente** por el río. Al subir al autocar, Robert dice —Vamos a volver por otro **camino.** Y pasar por el centro exacto de España que es el Cerro de los Angeles.
—¡Ay!—interrumpe Olwen—aquí está mi libro.
Bronwen ríe —¡Qué memoria tiene mi hermana!

49

VOCABULARIO

A.

el árbol	the tree
el camino	the way
la cara	the face
la cerveza	the beer
debajo de	under(neath), below
dejar	to leave (behind), to leave (off)
delante de	in front of
despertar(ie)	to wake
dormir(ue)	to sleep
elegir(i)	to choose
entre	among
el huevo	the egg
el jamón	the ham
leer	to read
lentamente	slowly
el libro	the book
luego	then, later
la máquina (fotográfica)	the camera
la merienda	the picnic meal
la naranja	the orange
el pan	the bread - *loaf*
para	(in order) to
el periódico	the newspaper
el plátano	the banana
el pueblo	the small town, the village
el queso	the cheese
reír (i)	to laugh
servir(i)	to serve
sobre	on (top of)
sonreír(i)	to smile

B. Expressions:

lo siento	I'm sorry
pasar el rato	to pass the time
situado al borde del río . . .	situated on the River . . .

GRAMATICA

38. **Radical-changing Verbs,** 3rd group, **e** to **i.**

Pedir   *to ask for*
pido
pides
pide
pedimos
pedís
piden

Note:
pedir, to ask for; preguntar, to ask (a question).

39. **Possessive Pronouns.** These agree in number and gender with the nouns they represent. The definite article may be omitted only after the verb **ser.**

el mío, la mía, los míos, las mías	mine
el tuyo, la tuya, los tuyos, las tuyas	yours
el suyo, la suya, los suyos, las suyas	his, hers, its, yours
el nuestro, la nuestra, los nuestros, las nuestras	ours
el vuestro, la vuestra, los vuestros, las vuestras	yours
el suyo, la suya, los suyos, las suyas	theirs, yours

Examples:
Tengo mi libro y tienes el tuyo.
I have my book and you have yours.
Comemos nuestras meriendas y coméis las vuestras.
We eat our snacks and you eat yours.
No es su revista, es mía.
It is not her magazine, it is mine.

Where the meaning of **suyo** is not clear, the forms **de él, de ella,** etc. may be substituted or added.

Example:
La máquina es (suya) de él pero las fotografías son (suyas) de ella.
The camera is his but the photographs are hers.

40. **Adverbs.** These are regularly formed by adding **-mente** to the FEMININE SINGULAR form of the adjective. An accent on an adjective is retained on the corresponding adverb.

Examples:

Adjective	*Adverb*
preciso	precisamente
estupendo	estupendamente
usual	usualmente
rápido	rápidamente

When two adverbs are used to modify the same verb, only the second one adds **-mente,** e.g. **trabaja lenta y precisamente.** Some common adverbs not ending in **-mente** have already been met, e.g. **temprano**—*early,* **bastante**—*enough, fairly, rather.*

41. **Al + infinitive** is the equivalent of *on + gerund.*

Examples:
Al ver el dinero están contentos.
On seeing the money they are glad.
Al entrar en el hotel ven a sus amigas.
On entering the hotel they see their friends.

EJERCICIOS

1. Form regular adverbs from the following adjectives and give their meanings.
      exacto; natural; contento; magnífico; general; nuevo; severo; último; usual; típico.

2. Make the possessive pronoun in brackets agree.
    (a) Esta casa es (mío), ésa es (tuyo).
    (b) Aquí están mis libros. ¿Dónde están (el tuyo)?
    (c) Pedro come bocadillos. Los bocadillos son (suyo).
    (d) No queremos las revistas de Mamá. Queremos (el nuestro).
    (e) La pelota es de Pablo. Es (suyo).

3. Put in the possessive pronouns.
    (a) ¿Es de Anita este paquete? No, no es . . .
    (b) ¿Tiene Elena su mapa? Sí, tiene . . .

(c) ¿Lee Ramón el libro de Vd.? Sí, lee . . .
(d) Aquí están mis billetes. ¿Dónde están . . .?
(e) Ella saca sus entradas. Yo saco . . .
(f) ¿Son de los niños las pesetas? Sí, son . . .
(g) Niños, ésas no son vuestras pelotas. Aquí están . . .
(h) La casa es de los Sánchez. Es . . .
(i) Quiero ver a mi madre y tú quieres ver a . . .
(j) Nosotros tenemos muchas sillas. Las sillas son . . .

4. Translate into Spanish:
(a) The children ask for bread.
(b) "What time is it?" asks the boy.
(c) I'm sorry but I don't want it.
(d) On arriving in Madrid we go to our hotel.
(e) Pepe is reading a magazine in order to pass the time.
(f) That house over there is theirs.
(g) We usually go early in order to see the teacher.
(h) The teacher speaks rapidly and precisely.
(i) He sleeps beneath a tree.
(j) After eating they read their books.

5. Answer the questions:
(a) ¿Dónde está Aranjuez?
(b) ¿Qué hacen los Evans allí?
(c) ¿A qué hora comen los Evans?
(d) ¿Qué comen?
(e) ¿Quién sirve la merienda?
(f) ¿Por qué no tienen que hablar tanto las niñas?
(g) ¿Cómo vuelven a Madrid los turistas?
(h) ¿Cuándo vuelven?
(i) ¿Por qué ríe Bronwen en el autocar?
(j) ¿Dónde está el cerro de los Angeles?

6. Translate into Spanish:
On Wednesday the English tourists make another excursion. They go to Aranjuez. On arriving in the town they walk to the river and go by boat to the palace. They travel slowly between the trees. The two sisters take their cameras. One takes many photographs with hers but the other prefers to sunbathe and read her paper. When their mother serves the picnic lunch the girls say they are not hungry but both ask for fruit and lemonade.

LECCION 10

VAN DE COMPRAS

El jueves las cuatro profesoras **van de compras**. **Desayunan temprano** y salen antes de las nueve. Quieren comprar **recuerdos** y **regalos**. **Van a pie** a Galerías Preciados, **almacén** muy grande. A la señorita Chester le **gustan los pañuelos** y **los manteles bordados**. A la señorita York le gusta **un vestido azul, talla** 40, que compra. También compra **unos zapatos blancos**, número 38. A la señorita Lancaster le gustan **las muñecas** y **los abanicos**. Y la señorita Stafford compra **juguetes** porque tiene muchos **sobrinos**. Ella sabe que a ellos les gustan los regalos de otros **países**.

Al salir del almacén van a un café para tomar té con limón. Hay **un limpiabotas** que trabaja en el café y las señoritas ven que **limpia** solamente los zapatos **negros** y **marrones** de los señores. También trabaja **fuera** del café un vendedor de cigarrillos y un vendedor de la Lotería Nacional. Los dos son **ciegos**.

Buscan una farmacia para comprar aspirinas y una perfumería para comprar **jabón** y **crema bronceadora**.

En otro almacén la señorita Chester compra **una falda color rosa**. A sus amigas les gusta mucho la falda.

—Me gusta también este sueter **color naranja**—dice la señorita Chester—pero no tengo más dinero.

—**Además,** aunque las tiendas no cierran hasta la una y media, tenemos que volver temprano al hotel porque hoy comemos a la una y salimos para El Escorial a las dos.

—¡Caramba! Es la una menos cuarto.

Las señoritas toman un taxi. Los taxis madrileños son negros con **una raya roja** y cuando están **libres** llevan **una luz verde**. En España un viaje en taxi es bastante barato. Las señoritas **pagan** veinte pesetas. Entran en el comedor a la una **en punto**.

VOCABULARIO

A.

el abanico	the fan
además	besides
el almacén	department store
bordado	embroidered
buscar	to look for
ciego	blind
crema bronceadora	suntan cream
desayunar	to have breakfast
la falda	the skirt
fuera de	outside
gustar	to like
el jabón	the soap
el juguete	the toy
libre	free
el limpiabotas	the bootblack
limpiar	to clean
la luz	the light
el mantel	the tablecloth
la muñeca	the doll
pagar	to pay
el país	the country
el pañuelo	the handkerchief
para	for (destination)
la raya	the stripe
el recuerdo	the souvenir
el regalo	the gift
el sobrino	the nephew
la talla	the size
temprano	early
el vestido	the dress
el zapato	the shoe

B. Expressions:

Ir de compras	to go shopping
Ir a pie	to go on foot
En punto	on the dot

C. Los Colores:

negro	black

blanco	white
marrón	brown
gris	grey
rojo	red
amarillo	yellow
verde	green
azul	blue
de color naranja	orange
de color rosa	pink

Note:
Adjectives of colour agree with the noun, but note **de color naranja** and **de color rosa.**

Examples:
La falda es negra.
Los zapatos son marrones.
but
El libro es de color rosa.

GRAMATICA

42. Indirect Object Pronouns:

me	to me
te	to you
le	to him
le	to her
le	to it
le	to you (Vd.)
nos	to us
os	to you
les	to them (m)
les	to them (f)
les	to you (Vds.)

The indirect object pronouns normally come before the verb.

Examples:
La profesora **nos** da el abanico. The teacher gives the
    fan *to us.*

El guía **les** habla. The guide speaks *to them.*
To avoid ambiguity or to add emphasis, the prepositional
forms, **a él, a ella, a Vd., a ellos, a ellas, a Vds.** may
be added.

Example:
 Les das el pañuelo **a ellas.** You (fam. sing.) give the
 handkerchief to them (fem. plural).

43. **Gustar**—to like, to be fond of.
 This verb is used in the 3rd person singular and 3rd
 person plural ONLY. It is used in the sense of *to be
 pleasing.* The subject of gustar FOLLOWS the verb.

Examples:
 Me gusta la falda. I like the skirt (the skirt is pleasing
 to me).

Note:
 She likes them but I do not like them.
This could be translated by **Le gustan pero no me
gustan.** This however, would not emphasise the contrast.
In order to make this emphasis the disjunctive pronouns
are added.
 Le gustan a ella pero no me gustan a mí.

EJERCICIOS

1. Use the indirect object pronouns instead of the words in
 brackets:
 (a) El ciego vende los billetes (a las profesoras).
 (b) El ciego vende los billetes (al guía).
 (c) La señorita contesta (a su amiga).
 (d) La señora contesta (a sus sobrinos).
 (e) El limpiabotas da el zapato (a los señores).
 (f) El limpiabotas da el zapato (al hombre).
 (g) El médico habla (a los niños).
 (h) El médico habla (al vendedor).
 (i) Dice (a Robert) que sí.
 (j) Dice (a la señorita Chester) que sí.

2. Answer the following questions using **gustar**:
    (a) ¿Te gusta el té? Sí, ...
    (b) ¿A Vd. le gusta España? Sí, ...
    (c) ¿A las profesoras les gustan los cigarrillos? No, ...
    (d) ¿A Vds. les gusta ir de compras? Sí, ...
    (e) ¿Le gusta a Robert ir a pie? No, ...

3. Translate the following sentences:
    (a) I like embroidered handkerchiefs.
    (b) Miss Chester and Miss Lancaster like to go shopping.
    (c) We like the meals in the hotel.
    (d) He does not like wine.
    (e) The children like the toys.
    (f) Do you like tea with lemon?
    (g) I like the blue dress.
    (h) She likes the green skirt.
    (i) Do you (vosotros) like the tablecloth?
    (j) They like the doll with the pink hat.

4. Translate into Spanish:
    I have breakfast early and go shopping. I buy presents at the department store. I like the pretty fans and the embroidered handkerchiefs. I buy aspirins at the chemist's shop. Then I have tea with lemon at a café. The shops close at half-past one. At one o'clock I take a taxi and return to the hotel.

5. With reference to the lesson, say whether the following statements are correct or incorrect.
    (a) Las cuatro profesoras desayunan temprano.
    (b) Las profesoras salen a las diez.
    (c) Van en taxi hasta una tienda pequeña.
    (d) El limpiabotas limpia los zapatos de las señoritas.
    (e) Viajar en taxi en España es muy caro.

6. CROSSWORD

ACROSS

1. The verb *to make*.
4. The verb *to believe*.
5. The months of December and January are usually this.
7. Transpose a list.
9. The month of showers.

DOWN

2. The verb *to open*.
3. Referred to in 5 across.
5. An article of clothing for women—and Scots.
6. How to address—in short—a Spanish lady.
8. Not to be confused with *estar*.

LECCION 11

HAY QUE VER EL ESCORIAL

Los ingleses están de nuevo en el autocar, **de camino** a El Escorial, un pueblo en la sierra a 50 kilómetros de Madrid. Robert les habla con entusiasmo. —**Hay que** ver el palacio **del rey** Felipe II y el monasterio dedicado a San Lorenzo. Aquí en las montañas el aire es **tan** limpio que **la piedra** del edificio y los cuadros en él **quedan** exactemente como en **el siglo XVI. Merece la pena** verlo, Bill, ¿no es verdad? El conductor está de acuerdo. —**Conduzco por** este **mismo** camino con cada grupo de turistas y **de vez en cuando** les acompaño por el palacio y el monasterio. Lo que me gustan más son **las tumbas** . . .

—¡Hombre! —El guía le coge **del brazo.** —¡Cuidado! No quiero ver mi **propia** tumba.

Bill sonríe. —**Chico**, ya sabes que conozco esta **carretera** con **los ojos cerrados.**

—Sin embargo, los prefiero **abiertos**—. **Sigue** más tranquilamente. —Otro sitio que **sin duda** vale la pena visitar es el Valle de **los Caídos**, un poco más lejos en las montañas. No lo visitamos **juntos** pero hay excursiones de las agencias de viajes de Madrid.

— ¿**Cómo es** este Valle de los Caídos?

—Hay una basílica **dentro** de **la roca** y sobre ella **una cruz** tan **alta** que hay un ascensor dentro de ella y **una biblioteca** en los brazos. Es una obra magnífica. Es el monumento a los caídos de la Guerra Civil de 1936–1939. La tumba de José Antonio Primo de Rivera está en la basílica.

— ¿Son **caras** las excursiones?

—No, son baratas. El viaje no es **largo**, es **corto, nada** más que 60 kilómetros de Madrid. Es **fácil** ir durante un día libre.

— ¿**Cuál** es el día que tenemos libre?

—El domingo.

Bill interrumpe. Ya están Vds. en El Escorial, **sanos y salvos.**

VOCABULARIO

A.

abierto	open
alto	high, tall
la biblioteca	the library
el brazo	the arm
el caído	the fallen, victim of war
caro	expensive
la carretera	the (main) road
cerrado	closed
conducir	to drive
corto	short
la cruz	the cross
el chico	the boy, the lad
dentro	inside
fácil	easy
la guerra	the war
junto	together
largo	long
mismo	same, very
nada	nothing
el ojo	the eye
la piedra	the stone
por	along, through
propio	own
quedar	to remain, stay
el rey	the king
la roca	the rock
seguir(i)	to continue, to follow
el siglo	the century
tan	so
la tumba	the tomb
ya	already, now

B. Expressions:

¡Cuidado!	look out!
de camino	on the way
de vez en cuando	from time to time.
hay que	one must.
merecer *or* valer la pena	to be worth the trouble.

sano y salvo	safe and sound.
sin duda	without doubt.

C. Question Words:

¿cuál, cuáles?	which?
¿cómo es?	what is . . . like?

Note:

¿Cómo es Ramón?	What is Ramón like?
¿Cómo está Ramón?	How is Ramón?

D. Ordinal Numbers:

1st	primero	1°		6th	sexto	6°
2nd	segundo	2°		7th	séptimo	7°
3rd	tercero	3°		8th	octavo	8°
4th	cuarto	4°		9th	noveno	9°
5th	quinto	5°		10th	décimo	10°

The ordinal numbers used as adjectives agree in number and gender with the noun.

Examples:

durante la segunda semana	during the second week.
agosto, el octavo mes	August, the eighth month

When used BEFORE a masculine, singular noun, **primero** and **tercero** are apocopated to **primer** and **tercer.**

Examples:

el primer día	the first day
el tercer hijo	the third son

Ordinals above tenth are rarely used.

Examples:

el siglo V = el siglo quinto
el siglo XIX = el siglo diecinueve
Felipe II = Felipe Segundo
Alfonso XIII = Alfonso Trece.

GRAMATICA

44. **Orthographic-changing Verbs.**

In certain verbs, in order to keep the original sound in the stem, a spelling change is made.

Group I

Conocer   *to know, to be acquainted with*
    conozco
    conoces
    conoce
    conocemos
    conocéis
    conocen

Similarly: conduzco—I drive; merezco—I deserve;
obedezco—I obey; parezco—I seem.

Note:
conocer   to know *people and places*
saber   to know *facts*

Group II

Coger   *to grasp, to hold*
    cojo
    coges
    coge
    cogemos
    cogéis
    cogen

Similarly: protejo—I protect; correjo—I correct.

45. **Direct Object Pronouns:**

me	me
te	you
lo *or* le	him, you (masc.)
la	her, you, it
lo	it, him
nos	us
os	you
los *or* les	them, you
las	them, you

(a) The direct object pronouns, like the indirect, normally
precede the verb.

Examples:
Le veo cada día. I see *him* every day.
Nos siguen por la calle. They follow *us* along the
    street.

(b) In the case of an infinitive the object pronoun is attached to the end.

Example:
Yo sé hacer**lo**. I know how to do *it*.

(c) The indirect object pronoun precedes the direct.

Examples:
No **te los** doy. I am not giving *them to you*.
Quieren dar**noslo**. They want to give *it to us*.

(d) When both the direct and the indirect object pronouns are 3rd person, i.e. both begin with **l**, the first one (the indirect) changes to **se**, whatever its meaning.

Examples:
Se lo hago de vez en cuando. I do *it for them* from time to time.
Quiero leer**selo**. I want to read *it to her*.

(e) Object pronouns are frequently used where not strictly necessary.

Examples:
¿Le conoce a Manuel? Do you know Manuel?
Les escribo a los primos. I am writing to my cousins.

46. **The Definite Article instead of the Possessive Adjective.**

Strictly speaking, the definite article, rather than a possessive adjective is used with parts of the body, clothing, personal belongings and relations, although in practice this rule is often broken.

47. **Más que, más de.**

More than is translated by **más que** except when the second part of the comparison is a cardinal number or a clause, in which case **más de** is used.

Examples:
Es más alto que el profesor. He is taller than the teacher.
Tienen más de noventa. They have more than ninety.
Note the difference between:
No tengo **más de** veinte pesetas.
I have no more than twenty pesetas. (maybe less)

No tengo **más que** veinte pesetas.
I have only twenty pesetas. (exactly)

EJERCICIOS

1. Give the opposites:
   corto; lentamente; cerrado; bajar; sin; sobre; caro; arriba; aquí; limpio.
2. Put in the correct form of the verb in brackets:
   (a) Yo (merecer) más dinero.
   (b) Yo (proteger) a mis hijos.
   (c) Yo (obedecer) al profesor.
   (d) Yo (conducir) un autobús.
   (e) Yo (corregir) los ejercicios.
3. Change the object nouns into object pronouns and insert them in the correct position in the sentence:
   (a) No entendemos *el libro*.
   (b) Voy a escribir *la lista* ahora.
   (c) La madre lee *una revista a los niños*
   (d) Los profesores enseñan *el inglés a sus estudiantes*.
   (e) Visitan a *Ricardo y yo*.
4. Put into Spanish:
   (a) His friend grasps his arm.
   (b) We are living in the twentieth century.
   (c) Pepito is the first in his class.
   (d) Which is the third day of the week?
   (e) What is the library like?

LECCION 12

MORAG TIENE ONCE AÑOS

Hoy el grupo pasa el día en Madrid. No van de excursión. Las niñas de la familia Evans, Olwen y Bronwen, los niños de la familia Scott, Duncan y Morag, y los niños de la familia Brown, John y Janet, deciden ir a la piscina. Janet **se levanta** a las ocho. Va al cuarto de baño. Allí se lava **las manos**, la cara y **los dientes. Llama** a su hermano.

—¡**El agua** está **caliente** si quieres **bañarte**!

Al fin John se levanta perezosamente y va a bañarse. Janet termina de **vestirse** y **se peina**. Baja **la escalera** y va al comedor. En el comedor están los otros. Los niños **charlan**. Hoy es **el cumpleaños** de Morag. **Tiene once años**. Todos los niños le **traen** regalos. Duncan tiene sólo diez años pero es más alto que su hermana.

—¿Cuántos años tienes tú?—pregunta Morag a Olwen.

—Tengo nueve años y mi hermana tiene ocho años.

—Pero yo soy más inteligente que Olwen—ríe Bronwen.

—¿Crees tú? pregunta su hermana.

El camarero sirve **bollos** y **mantequilla, mermelada** y café con leche. **Aún** no está John. Duncan pregunta:

—¿Dónde está John?

—Está **todavía** en el cuarto de baño. Tiene mucho sueño esta mañana.

Duncan sube la escalera, **golpea** la puerta del cuarto de baño y dice:

—Ya son las nueve.

No hay **respuesta**. Duncan va a la habitación de John y llama:

—¿No te levantas? ¿Estás todavía en la cama?

—No, me peino pero no encuentro los zapatos.

Duncan entra.

—Aquí están los zapatos debajo de la cama.

—No veo **el billetero**.

Duncan busca el billetero.

66

—Aquí está en **el tocador.**

—No puedo abrir la puerta **del armario**—dice John. Al fin bajan al comedor y John se sienta a la mesa. Solamente toma café con leche. No le queda tiempo para comer.

VOCABULARIO

A.

el agua	the water
el armario	the wardrobe
aún	yet
bañarse	to take a bath
el billetero	the wallet
el bollo	the roll
caliente	hot
el camarero	the waiter
el cumpleaños	the birthday
charlar	to chat
los dientes	the teeth
encontrar	to find, to meet
la escalera	the staircase
golpear	to knock
levantarse	to get up
llamar	to call
la mano	the hand
la mantequilla	the butter
la mermelada	the jam
peinarse	to comb one's hair
la respuesta	the reply
sentarse	to sit down
el tocador	the dressing table
todavía	yet, still
traer	to bring
vestirse	to dress oneself

B. Stressed 'a' or 'ha'.

When a feminine noun begins with a stressed 'a' or 'ha' the masculine definite article is used for the sake of euphony. This applies in the singular only, e.g.

el agua *but* las aguas

el haba (the bean) *but* las habas.

68 SPANISH ONCE A WEEK

C. ¿Cuántos años? + tener.
Note this expression.

Examples:
¿Cuántos años tiene Roberto? How old is Robert?
Roberto tiene diez años, la hermana tiene ocho. Robert is ten, his sister is eight.

D. Omission of 'can'.
No encuentro mis zapatos. I can't find my shoes.
¿Ve Vd. a María? Can you see Maria?

GRAMATICA

48. **Reflexive Verbs** are very commonly used in Spanish. They are formed by placing the reflexive pronouns **me, te, se, nos, os, se** in front of the verb. These reflexive pronouns may be translated by *myself, yourself, himself, ourselves*, etc. but are often not expressed at all in English.

Lavarse *to wash oneself*
me lavo
te lavas
se lava
nos lavamos
os laváis
se lavan

The reflexive pronoun normally precedes the verb:
me lavo—I wash myself
but with an infinitive verb the pronoun follows and is joined to the verb:
voy a lavarme—I am going to wash myself.

Other reflexive verbs used so far include **levantarse, bañarse, vestirse, peinarse, sentarse.** These verbs are not always used reflexively.

Note:
Juan se lava. John washes himself.
Juan lava la camisa. John washes his shirt.

The Negative is formed by placing 'no' in front of the reflexive pronoun.

Example:
No me levanto hasta las nueve. I am not getting up
until nine o'clock.

The Interrogative is formed by altering the word order.

Example:
¿Se lava John? Does John wash himself?

A verb may have a different meaning when used reflexively, e.g.
ir—to go; irse—to go away; llamar—to call; llamarse—
to be named.

Examples:

Nos vamos ahora.	We are going away now.
¿A qué hora vamos?	What time are we going?
Llamo a Juan.	I am calling John.
Me llamo Juan.	I am called John.

49. **Regular Comparatives and Superlatives.**
Most adjectives are compared as follows:

	Comparative	*Superlative*
inteligente	más inteligente	(el) más inteligente
intelligent	more intelligent	the most intelligent

However when a noun being described is preceded by the
definite article, the article which precedes the superlative
adjective is omitted.

Example:
El niño más inteligente could mean the MORE
intelligent boy or the MOST intelligent boy.

Similarly:
menos; less, least.

Note:

más . . . que	more . . . than
menos . . . que	less . . . than
tan . . . como	as . . . as
tanto . . . como	as much, many . . . as

Examples:
Janet es más inteligente que John.
Janet tiene menos libros que John.
John no es tan inteligente como Janet.

50. **Three Irregular Verbs in the Present Indicative:**
traer—*to bring;* **caer**—*to fall;* **poder**—*to be able.*

traigo	caigo	puedo
traes	caes	puedes
trae	cae	puede
traemos	caemos	podemos
traéis	caéis	podéis
traen	caen	pueden

EJERCICIOS

1. Translate into Spanish:
   (a) I wash my hands.
   (b) Carmen is combing her hair.
   (c) He gets up at eight o'clock in the morning.
   (d) The children dress themselves.
   (e) Are you going away tomorrow?
   (f) Generally we take a bath in the morning.
   (g) How old are you? (tú)
   (h) His name is José.
   (i) Can you (Vd.) see my book?
   (j) Do you (Vds.) want to sit here?

2. Replace the infinitive, in brackets, by the appropriate part of the verb.
   (a) Juan no (poder) (venir) hoy.
   (b) El camarero (traer) el café a la mesa.
   (c) Yo (caer) porque (estar) cansado.
   (d) Nosotros (poder) (irse) mañana.
   (e) Yo le (traer) el libro.

3. Translate into Spanish:
   (a) He has more friends than I.
   (b) She is not as smart as her sister.
   (c) John is more intelligent than his brother.
   (d) He has fewer pesetas than his friend.
   (e) I am bigger than my cousin.

4. Answer in Spanish, the following questions:
   (a) ¿A qué hora se levanta Janet?
   (b) ¿Qué hace Janet en el cuarto de baño?
   (c) ¿Se baña John?

(d) ¿Por qué traen regalos los niños?
(e) ¿Cuántos años tiene Duncan?
(f) ¿Es Morag más grande que Duncan?
(g) ¿Qué sirve el camarero?
(h) ¿Dónde está John?
(i) ¿Por qué se levanta tarde esta mañana?
(j) ¿Por qué toma café con leche solamente?

LECCION 13

NO PUEDO MAS

Los turistas esperan al guía.
—¿No viene Robert?
—Sí, aquí está.
El guía **explica** el itinerario. —¿Me oyen Vds? Bueno.
Primero viajamos en el Metro hasta la estación final que se llama Argüelles. **Desde** la estación los turistas van por la Calle Princesa. Miran el edificio del Ministerio del Aire. Este es una réplica moderna de El Escorial. Delante del ministerio se ven **unos jardines bellos** con **bancos,** fuentes y un estanque. Hace muchísimo calor. John, el menor de los niños, **se quita** las sandalias y **mete** los pies en el agua.
—¡Dios mío!—dice su madre. —¡Qué niño más **travieso**!
Siguen hasta el Arco de la Victoria, monumento altísimo, tan alto que la gente **parece** tan pequeña como muñecas. **Luego,** cogen **un tranvía** para ver **sin trabajo** la Ciudad Universitaria donde se encuentran todas las Facultades y residencias de la Universidad de Madrid. Admiran la ciudad que es **ancha** y verde y les gustan especialmente la Facultad de Filosofía y Letras y el Museo de América.
Después de bajar del tranvía y merendar, suben al autobús para ir a El Pardo, donde vive el Generalísimo Franco en una gran casa **rodeada** por **una valla.** En todas las puertas se encuentran **soldados montados** a **caballo.** Los soldados se charlan pero al ver la máquina de la señorita York, uno de ellos **grita:**
—¡No, señora, se prohibe sacar fotografías aquí!
Los niños **maravillan** de **los fusiles** de los soldados pero los mayores prefieren la Casita del Príncipe donde hay **muebles** y **relojes** franceses.
Vuelven por la Casa de Campo donde va la gente de la capital para **divertirse.** Hay un bonito lago y una piscina.

Además es un sitio ideal para ir a caballo. Pero los ingleses están cansadísimos. Solamente pueden sentarse y mirar.
—Papá, ¿qué vamos a hacer ahora?—pregunta John.
—¡Hombre! **No puedo más.**

VOCABULARIO

A.

ancho	wide
el banco	the seat
bello	beautiful
el caballo	the horse
desde	from
divertirse (ie)	to enjoy oneself
explicar	to explain
el fusil	the rifle
gritar	to shout
el jardín	the garden
luego	then, later
maravillar	to admire
meter	to put
montado	mounted
el mueble	a piece of furniture
parecer	to seem
el príncipe	the prince
quitarse	to take off, to remove
el reloj	the clock
rodeado (por)	surrounded (by)
el soldado	the soldier
el tranvía	the tram
travieso	naughty
la valla	the fence, stockade

B. Expressions:
No puedo más. I can't do, take anything more.
Sin trabajo. Easily, without effort.

GRAMATICA

15. **Irregular Comparison of Adjectives.**
    There are a few adjectives in Spanish which compare irregularly.

Positive	*Comparative*	*Superlative*
pequeño	menor	el menor
small	smaller	the smallest
grande	mayor	el mayor
big	bigger	the biggest
bueno	mejor	el mejor
good	better	the best
malo	peor	el peor
bad	worse	the worst

(i) The irregular comparatives have the same form for both masculine and feminine.

(ii) **Mejor** and **peor** generally precede the noun.

Examples:

Los mejores estudiantes.   The best students.
La peor cosa.   The worst thing.

(iii) **Mayor** and **menor**, relating to persons, usually mean *older* and *younger* and follow the noun. When relating to things they mean *larger* and *smaller* and usually precede the noun.

Examples:

Mi hermano mayor.   My older brother.
La mayor parte.   The larger part.

Note:

Pequeño and **grande** may also be compared regularly. The regular form generally refers to physical size.

52. **Absolute Superlative of Adjectives and Adverbs.**

In order to express the absolute superlative we may add **-ísimo(s) -ísima(s)** to the stem of the adjective or adverb. This form is widely used in Spanish.

Examples:

Una chica hermosísima.   A most beautiful girl.
Muchísimas gracias.   Very many thanks.
Me levanto tempranísimo.   I get up very early.

When a superlative adjective is followed by *in*, it is translated by **de**, e.g. **el edificio más alto del mundo**—*the tallest building in the world.*

Sometimes a change of spelling is necessary when **ísimo** is added, in order to keep the same sound.

Examples:

rico (rich)   riquísimo (very rich)
feliz (happy)   felicísimo (very happy)

53. **Three More Irregular Verbs in the Present Indicative.**

Oír *to hear*	**Venir** *to come*
oigo	vengo
oyes	vienes
oye	viene
oímos	venimos
oís	venís
oyen	vienen

Poner *to put*
pongo
pones
pone
ponemos
ponéis
ponen

Note:

Poner is irregular in the first person singular only.

54. **Further Uses of the Reflexive "se".**

(a) **Reciprocal Verbs.** These use the same form as the reflexive verbs but in this case the pronouns have the meaning of *each other, one another.*

Examples:

Nos vemos todos los días. We see each other every day.

Se quieren mucho. They love one another very much.

(b) **The Passive Voice** is often translated by a reflexive verb.

Examples:

Se prohibe sacar fotografías. Taking photographs is prohibited.

Aquí se habla español. Spanish spoken here.
Se dice que está enfermo. It is said that he is ill.
Se bebe mucho café en Francia. A lot of coffee is
drunk in France.

EJERCICIOS

1. Translate into Spanish:
   (a) Juan's house is small, but his sister's house is smaller.
   (b) Conchita is older than José, but she is smaller.
   (c) The boy is not as tired as his father.
   (d) I have not as many toys as Pedro.
   (e) This book is the worst of all.
   (f) My brother is younger than I.
   (g) María and Pilar are the youngest.
   (h) The best fruit is on the table.
   (i) He is a good student but his sister is better.
   (j) The best student is María.
2. Replace the infinitive by the correct part of the verb:
   (a) Carlos y yo (venir) hoy.
   (b) Las profesoras (poner) los libros en la mesa.
   (c) Yo (venir) todos los días.
   (d) ¿(Oír) bien Vds?
   (e) Yo (oír) muy bien, pero Carmen no (oír) tan bien.
3. Translate into Spanish:
   (a) What a naughty girl!
   (b) He takes off his hat.
   (c) Mr. Brown is a very good architect indeed.
   (d) They write to one another every week.
   (e) That's enough, I can't take any more.
   (f) I'm sorry, I can't hear.
   (g) They say he is very, very rich.
   (h) English is spoken here.
   (i) Besides the furniture there are the most beautiful French
       clocks.
   (j) The prince and princess ride big black horses.
4. Finish the sentences with a few more words:
   (a) El Ministerio del Aire es . . .
   (b) Se dice que . . .

(c) El niño se quita . . .
(d) La hija menor . . .
(e) Viajan en tranvía hasta . . .
(f) No es tan . . .
(g) Hay tantos . . .
(h) Sacan muchísimas . . .
(i) Se prohibe . . .
(j) La piscina está . . .

5. The initial letters of the answers to the clues form a new word which is **un sitio para nadar y tomar el sol.**

. . .   Puerta principal.
. . .   País más grande de la Gran Bretaña.
. . .   Hombres militares.
. . .   Hablar de cosas no muy importantes.
. . .   País de San Patricio.
. . .   No es viejo, es . . .
. . .   En este momento.

LECCION 14

¡CHUTA!

Esta noche se **celebra un partido** de fútbol entre los dos **equipos** más famosos de Madrid, el Atlético de Madrid y el Real Madrid. Naturalmente, los dos futbolistas ingleses **se interesan** mucho. **Les interesa cualquier** partido pero **tienen muchas ganas** de ver a estos equipos tan **célebres.** Invitan a Robert pero no quiere ir. No va **nunca** al fútbol. No tiene **ningún** interés. Peter y Philip deciden ir en el Metro porque **anda** más **de prisa** que el antobús. **El Estadio** Bernabéu está **lleno** de gente. Afortunadamente, quedan **algunos** bancos **vacíos.**

—Mira—dice Philip, después de sentarse —Venden **churros.** ¿Quieres?

—Sí. Tráeme un cucurucho grande.

Philip se va. Un minuto más tarde Peter le grita:

—Oye, Philip, tráeme dos cucuruchos, y un programa y **date prisa,** que va a empezar el partido.

—Bueno, bueno. Espera un momento.

El partido es estupendo. Los defensas del Real Madrid son magníficos pero **los delanteros** Atléticos driblan y **chutan** más **hábilmente** que los del otro equipo. Peter y Philip gritan con **los demás aficionados.**

—¡Chuta!

—¡**Una falta!** ¡Echale!

—¡Corred!

Por el entusiasmo unos españoles se levantan y sus amigos de detrás les gritan:

—¡Sentaos! ¡Dejadnos ver!

Todo el mundo se divierte, los dos futbolistas ingleses más que **nadie.** Miran el gran estadio y **se preguntan si** un día vienen a jugar a él.

Al fin el Atlético de Madrid **gana** 3–2.

—Y ahora ¿qué?—pregunta Peter. — ¿Vamos a algún bar?

—Sí, vamos. Tengo sed después de gritar tanto.

—Eso no me **sorprende**. Eres peor que nuestros aficionados en Inglaterra. Mañana va a **dolerte la garganta.**

—Si a mí me duele la garganta mañana, **lo mismo** les va a **pasar** a miles de madrileños. Pero no **importa**, merece la pena. Son dos equipos maravillosos.

—De acuerdo. Vamos, **te invito** a una cerveza.

VOCABULARIO

A.

aficionado	the devotee
algún	some
andar	to go (mechanically)
celebrar	to celebrate
célebre	famous
cualquier	any (at all)
el cucurucho	the paper cone
el churro	a kind of fritter
el delantero	the forward
los demás	the rest, remaining
de prisa	quickly
doler (ue)	to ache
echar	to throw out
el equipo	the team
el estadio	the stadium
la falta	the foul
ganar	to win
hábilmente	cleverly
interesar(se)	to interest, to be interested in
lleno	full
el partido	the match
pasar	to happen
preguntarse	to wonder
si	whether
vacío	empty

B. Expressions:

darse prisa	to hurry up
me duele la garganta, la cabeza, etc.	I have a sore throat, headache, etc.

no importa	it doesn't matter
te invito	I'll treat you
tener ganas de (+ infinitive)	to have a desire to, to feel like

C. Negative Words:

nadie	nobody, no one
ningún	none (at all)
nunca	never

D. Neuter Nouns, i.e. adjectives preceded by neuter article, lo.

lo mismo	the same thing

Similarly:

lo importante	the important thing
lo mejor	the best thing

GRAMATICA

55. The Familiar Imperative.

Affirmative commands to those we address as *tú* and *vosotros* are shown below.

	-ar verbs	-er verbs	-ir verbs
2nd person singular	mira look!	corre run!	escribe write!
2nd person plural	mirad	corred	escribid

Some verbs have irregular familiar imperatives in the SINGULAR only.

Verb	Command	Example
hacer	haz	¡hazlo! do it!
ir	ve	¡vete! go away!
poner	pon	¡pon el sombrero! Put on your hat!
salir	sal	¡sal de prisa! Go out quickly!
tener	ten	¡ten cuidado! take care!
venir	ven	¡ven aquí! come here!

Note:

The object pronouns are attached to the end of these imperatives, usually necessitating an accent in the singular so that the verb retains its usual stress.

Examples:
¡Dámelos!	Give them to me!
¡Traedlo aquí!	Bring it here!

The plural command when followed by the object pronoun **os** loses its **d.**

Examples:
¡Sentaos!	Sit down!
¡Lavaos las manos!	Wash your hands!

The imperative form *let's* is translated by **vamos a.**

Examples:
¡Vamos a comer!	Let's eat!
¡Vamos a ver!	Let's see!

56. **Double Negatives.**

When a negative such as **nunca**—*never*, **nadie**—*nobody*, etc. follows the verb, the verb must be preceded by **no.**

Examples:
No va nadie.	Nobody is going.
No lo encuentro en ningún sitio.	I can't find it anywhere.
No como nunca el pan.	I never eat bread.

In some sentences, as an alternative to the double negative, the negative word may precede the verb.

Examples:
Nadie va.	Nobody is going.
Nunca como pan.	I never eat bread.

57. **Comparison of Adverbs.**

The regular comparison of adverbs follows the same pattern as that of adjectives.

Examples
hábilmente	más hábilmente	el más hábilmente
cleverly	more cleverly	most cleverly
de prisa	más de prisa	el más de prisa
quickly	more quickly	most quickly

Note the irregular comparisons of:
bien	mejor	el mejor
well	better	best

mal	peor	el peor
badly	worse	worst

58. Apocopation of Adjectives.

A few adjectives, in given circumstances, lose their final letters.

(a) Before a MASCULINE SINGULAR noun only:

bueno *becomes* buen

un buen hombre	a good chap

malo *becomes* mal

hace mal tiempo	it's bad weather

alguno *becomes* algún

algún día	some day

ninguno *becomes* ningún

no le gusta ningún vino	he likes no wine

primero *becomes* primer

el primer día	the first day

tercero *becomes* tercer

el tercer piso	the third floor

(b) Before ANY noun:

ciento *becomes* cien

cien revistas y cien libros	a hundred magazines and a hundred books

(c) Before ANY SINGULAR noun:

grande *becomes* gran

una gran casa	a fine house

cualquiera *becomes* cualquier

cualquier sitio	any place (at all)

Note:

The position of the adjective may alter its meaning.

una casa grande	a *big* house
una gran casa	a *fine* house, a *great* house
un hombre bueno	a (morally) good man
un buen hombre	a good (likeable) chap
un hombre pobre	a (financially) poor man
¡el pobre hombre!	the poor (unfortunate) fellow!
una película nueva	a (brand) new film
una nueva película	a new (different) film

EJERCICIOS

1. Put the commands into Spanish:
   (a) Bring me a lemonade.
   (b) Children, wash your hands.
   (c) Take care!
   (d) Do it now, Juanito.
   (e) Drink your milk, boys.
2. Write in Spanish, remembering the double negatives:
   (a) Nobody comes here.
   (b) I don't want anything.
   (c) We can't find the list anywhere.
   (d) The guide never goes to a football match.
   (e) They can't see anybody anywhere.
3. Complete each sentence by inserting an adverb from the list below:
   MEJOR MAL AFORTUNADAMENTE DE PRISA
   SOLAMENTE   LENTAMENTE   SEVERAMENTE
   BIEN HABILMENTE PEOR
   (a) El médico escribe . . .
   (b) El fútbolista juega . . .
   (c) El tren va . . .
   (d) Lo hago . . . que tú.
   (e) . . . no le hace daño.
   (f) Los abuelos andan . . .
   (g) El profesor habla . . . al niño travieso.
   (h) Nuestro equipo juega más . . . que el otro.
   (i) Me quedan . . . dos pesetas.
   (j) Nado mal pero la hermana nada aun . . .
4. Translate into Spanish:
   The first place we see is the fine stadium. The Spanish team plays better than the Italian one. One poor Italian falls and hurts his head. He is going to have a headache tomorrow. "Get up!" the Italian supporters shout at him, but he cannot. "Hurry up!" shouts everyone. "Let's see a bit of football!"

LECCION 15

¡QUE APROVECHE!

Al día **siguiente** los ingleses tienen que **madrugar.**
—Desayunen pronto—les dice Robert. —Tenemos que salir
en seguida.

Bill les lleva en el autocar hasta la Estación del Norte,
estación de **ferrocarril,** donde Robert saca **billetes de ida
y vuelta,** para Avila. Durante dos horas el tren sube hasta la
ciudad alta y **aislada** de Avila, única ciudad de Europa
todavía completamente **amurallada.** Los turistas encuentran
que es una capital **encantadora** de muchísimos conventos e
iglesias, calles **estrechas,** vistas bellas y una gran catedral.
Robert **enseña** a su grupo el interior del Convento de Santa
Teresa y, fuera de **las murallas,** los Cuatro Postes de la misma
santa.

Hoy, **en vez de** comer de bocadillos, los ingleses comen en
un restaurante que **da a** la ancha Plaza de Santa Teresa de
Jesús, desde donde ven la Puerta de San Vicente, **fuerte** y
enorme. Los camareros les sirven **entremeses, tortilla** de
patata, **de tercer plato truchas** frescas con pan y vino, y de
postre melón.

—**¡Que aprovechen¡**—les dicen los camareros, y sin duda
a los ingleses les gusta esta comida española.

Luego hacen otra pequeña excursión de siete u ocho kilómetros en autocar, **sobre todo** para ver el Calvario en Piedra.
Todos se maravillan de esta gran escultura.

Acaban de bajar de nuevo en la plaza cuando Robert dice
—Bueno, nos quedan nada más que 40 ó 50 minutos en Avila.
Seguramente, Vds. quieren **dar una vuelta** y mirar los
escaparates, pero, por favor, estén aquí, cerca de la Puerta de
San Vicente, a las cinco en punto. El tren sale a las cinco y
media y no nos espera.

—¿Lo oís, señoras?—dice el doctor Scott. —Mirad los
escaparates pero no compréis nada. **Por suerte** no os queda
tiempo para gastar ni una peseta.

VOCABULARIO

A.

aislado	isolated
amurallado	walled
el billete de ida y vuelta	the return ticket
enseñar	to show
los entremeses	the hors-d'oeuvre
estrecho	narrow
el ferrocarril	the railway
fuerte	strong
gastar	to spend
madrugar	to get up early
la muralla	the city wall
ni	not even
el postre	the dessert
seguramente	probably, surely
siguiente	following
la tortilla	the omelette
la trucha	the trout

B. Expressions:

acabar de + infinitive	to have just + infinitive
acabo de llegar	*I have just arrived*
de primer/segundo/tercer plato	for first/second/third course
en seguida	at once
en vez de	instead of
por suerte	luckily
¡que aproveche!	the equivalent of the French *bon appétit!*
sobre todo	above all

C. Expressions with **dar**:

In addition to **dar un paseo**—*to take a walk* and **darse prisa**—*to hurry up* there are a number of common expressions using the verb **dar**.

dar a	to give onto
dar con	to meet accidentally, to bump into
dar de comer	to feed

> darse cuenta de   to realise
> dar una vuelta   to take a turn (round the block)

D. The feminine adjective **encantadora** belongs to a small group in which the masculine ends in **-or.**

encantador, encantadora	charming
malgastador, malgastadora	wasteful
trabajador, trabajadora	hard-working

GRAMATICA

59. **The Polite Imperative and Familiar Imperative (Negative).**

For these commands the subjunctive form is used. The present subjunctive is formed by taking the stem of the 1st person singular, present indicative, and adding the -ar endings to the -er and -ir verbs, and the -er endings to the -ar verbs.

Examples:

Hablar	Comer	Subir
hable	coma	suba
hables	comas	subas
hable	coma	suba
hablemos	comamos	subamos
habléis	comáis	subáis
hablen	coman	suban

Note:

1st person singular endings are the same as 3rd person singular.

Further Examples:

vengo, tengo, hago, etc. *become* venga, tenga, haga, etc.
obedezco, conduzco, cojo, etc. *become* obedezca, conduzca, coja, etc.

Radical-changing verbs keep the same stem pattern in the subjunctive as in the indicative.

puedo, pueda; quiero, quiera.

Irregulars:

ir   voy   vaya, vayas, vaya, vayamos, vayáis, vayan
ser   soy   sea, seas, sea, seamos, seáis, sean.

Commands:

For negative familiar commands use the 2nd persons of the subjunctive.

Examples:

¡No hagas eso!   Don't do that!
¡No comáis ésos!   Don't eat those!

For all polite commands use the 3rd persons of the subjunctive.

Examples:

¡Vengan aquí!   Come here!
Pase, por favor.   Please come in.
¡No me diga!   Don't tell me!
No trabajéis tanto.   Don't work so hard.

Note:

Vd. Vds. may be added to polite commands.
Tome Vd.   Take one, help yourself.
¡Miren Vds.!   Look!

Note:

The further uses of the subjunctive, which in Spanish are numerous, are beyond the scope of this elementary course.

60. **Alternative Forms** of **y** *and,* **o** *or.*

For convenience in pronunciation **y** becomes **e** before a word beginning with **i, hi** (but not **hie**) and **o** becomes **u** before a word beginning with **o, ho.**

ríos e islas   rivers and islands
agrícola e industrial   agricultural and industrial
belgo u holandés   Belgian or Dutch
de plata u oro   silver or gold

In addition the word **o** *or* placed between figures bears an accent to avoid confusion with zero.

10 ó 12 días   ten or twelve days
3 ó 4 meses   three or four months
300 ó 400 sellos   three or four hundred stamps

7

61. Durante.

Expressions such as *for* six weeks, *for* a long time are translated with **durante** *during*.

durante seis semanas
durante mucho tiempo

EJERCICIOS

1. Answer the questions in Spanish:
   (a) ¿Por qué tienen que madrugar los ingleses?
   (b) ¿Cómo van a la estación de ferrocarril?
   (c) ¿Cómo se llama la estación?
   (d) ¿Adónde van los ingleses?
   (e) ¿Cómo es Avila?
   (f) ¿Qué comen los ingleses?
   (g) ¿Qué les dicen los camareros?
   (h) ¿Por qué hacen los turistas otra pequeña excursión?
   (i) ¿A qué hora sale el tren para Madrid?
   (j) ¿Por qué dice el doctor Scott «por suerte»?

2. Use the expressions in sentences of your own:
   acabar de   darse cuenta de   dar a   ¡que aproveche!
   en vez de

3. Translate the commands into Spanish:
   (a) Look, gentlemen, here is the church.
   (b) Don't do that, child.
   (c) Mummy, buy one for me.
   (d) Show me the suitcases, sir.
   (e) Children, don't eat those dirty sweets.
   (f) Don't go in, madam.
   (g) Waiter, bring me a beer.
   (h) Sit down, ladies.
   (i) Go away, Juanito, and wash your hands and face.
   (j) Drive with care.

4. Write in Spanish:
   (a) They are travelling in Great Britain and Ireland.
   (b) For six months the weather is good.
   (c) He has seven or eight brothers and sisters.
   (d) I'm going to take a turn round the block while it is sunny.

(e) We have just realised that he is not here.
(f) They are hard-working people.
(g) Go to the other booking office, sir.
(h) There are 50 or 60 bedrooms in this hotel.
(i) He is a charming boy.
(j) What is there for the second course?

LECCION 16

NO SE PREOCUPE

El domingo por la mañana unos turistas fueron a varias iglesias de Madrid. Los católicos **oyeron misa** en la Catedral de San Isidro, patrón de la ciudad mientras algunos protestantes se interesaron por visitar una iglesia protestante de España. **Resultó difícil cantar** los himnos en español. El doctor Scott lleva a su familia a la Iglesia de San Jorge, de la **Embajada** Británica. Fue interesante ver al cónsul y al embajador y, después del oficio religioso, tomar **jerez** en el jardín.

—¡Es un jerez muy bueno!—exclamó el doctor.

—¿Pero cuándo vamos al **mercado**?—preguntó Duncan.

—En seguida—respondió su padre.

Fueron en taxi hasta la parte antigua de la capital donde está el mercado célebre, del Rastro.

—Vine aquí como estudiante—declaró el doctor.

—¿Qué venden en estos **puestos**?—preguntó su hija.

—Tales mercados siempre venden de todo; cosas como **antigüedades**, muebles, curiosidades, objetos usados, cuadros. Y no solamente eso sino libros, revistas, caramelos y **globos**.

Los niños compraron globos y caramelos y un toro de porcelana **para** los abuelos. Después de **vacilar** durante mucho tiempo entre dos relojes antiguos los padres decidieron comprar el más pequeño y el más barato **por el peso y la aduana**.

—¿Qué hora es?—preguntó la señora, con el paquete en las manos.

—¡Dios mío! Son las tres. **Debemos** estar en el comedor.

Buscaron un taxi. Pero fue difícil encontrar un taxi libre.

—¿**Qué pasa**?—preguntó la señora.

—Que es domingo y el domingo es fiesta. ¡Mira cuanta gente hay!

—Entonces ¿qué hacemos?

—Voy a llamar por teléfono al hotel.

Entró en un bar, compró **una ficha** y llamó el hotel.

—Hotel Santo Domingo. **Dígame.**

— **¿Está** el señor Robert Kay de la agencia 'Sunnidays'?

— **¿De parte de quién?**

—Del doctor Scott.

—Un momento. **Ahora mismo** le llamo.

Al cabo de unos minutos el médico le explicó todo al guía.

—**No se preocupe,** doctor. Vuelvan Vds. tranquilamente.

Yo voy a pedir una comida para Vds. y los niños a las cuatro.

¡Menos mal que no van a **la corrida de toros!**

VOCABULARIO

A.

la aduana	the Customs
la antigüedad	the antique
cantar	to sing
la corrida de toros	the bullfight
deber	ought, must
difícil	difficult
la embajada	the embassy
la ficha	the token
el globo	the (toy) balloon
el jerez	the sherry
el mercado	the market
el peso	the weight
por	on account of
preocuparse	to worry
el puesto	the stall
resultar	to turn out
vacilar	to hesitate

B. Expressions:

ahora mismo	this very minute
al cabo de	after (+ a period of time)
no se preocupe	never mind, don't worry
(familiar—no te preocupes)	
oír misa	to hear mass
¿qué pasa?	what's happening? *Also*
¿qué te pasa?	what's the matter with you?

C. The Telephone:

Dígame *literally* tell me, said on lifting receiver.

Está Miguel? Is Miguel in? Is Miguel there?

¿De parte de quién? On whose behalf?

GRAMATICA

62. The Preterite (Past Definite) Tense.

The preterite is used to express single, definite, completed actions in the past. The regular endings are as follows.

Cantar *to sing*		**Correr** *to run*		**Decidir** *to decide*	
canté	*I sang*	corrí	*I ran*	decidí	*I decided*
cantaste		corriste		decidiste	
cantó		corrió		decidió	
cantamos		corrimos		decidimos	
cantasteis		corristeis		decidisteis	
cantaron		corrieron		decidieron	

Notes:

The **-er** and **-ir** endings are identical. In **-ar** and **-ir** verbs the 1st person plural endings of the preterite and the present indicative are the same.

Where an unaccented **i** would occur between two vowels a **y** is substituted, e.g. in **caer**—*to fall*, **leer**—*to read*, **oír**—*to hear*.

caí	leí	oí
caíste	leíste	oíste
cayó	**leyó**	**oyó**
caímos	leímos	oímos
caísteis	leísteis	oísteis
cayeron	**leyeron**	**oyeron**

Irregular Preterite of **ser** and **ir**.

Ser and **ir** have identical preterites.

Ser		**Ir**	
fui	*I was*	fui	*I went*
fuiste		fuiste	
fue		fue	
fuimos		fuimos	

SPANISH ONCE A WEEK

93

fuisteis   fuisteis
fueron   fueron

63. **Pero and Sino.**

But is translated by **pero** when the conjunction joins two separate statements. When *but* follows a negative statement and the second statement is in opposition it is translated by **sino**.

Example:

No son tuyos sino míos.   They are not yours but mine.
No estudio francés sino   I don't study French but
    alemán.   German.

64. **Tal, tales.**

While **tan** such a qualifies an adjective, **tal** and **tales** with the same meaning qualify a noun.

Examples:

Tal hombre es útil.   Such a man is useful.
No debe creer tales cosas.   You mustn't believe such
                       things.

65. **The Diaeresis.**

Occasionally, to preserve the **w** sound, rather than the hard **g,** the **u** in **gue** and **gui** is marked with a diaeresis, **güe, güi.**

Study:

antiguo (ancient)   la antigüedad (the antique)
vergonzoso (shameful)   la vergüenza (the shame)

EJERCICIOS

1. Put the verb in brackets into the preterite tense:
   (a) El inglés (hablar) con la recepcionista.
   (b) Los niños (correr) por las calles.
   (c) El médico (tomar) una copa de jerez.
   (d) El domingo mi amigo (oír) misa en la catedral.
   (e) (Ser) muy difícil encontrar un taxi libre.
   (f) Yo no (vacilar) ni un momento.
   (g) Margarita (leer) la carta con cuidado.
   (h) Los americanos (ir) a la Embajada.

(i) Tú (cantar) muy bien.

(j) Vosotros (comer) la naranja en el parque.

2. Write in Spanish:

    (a) He arrived at half past seven.

    (b) We bought several pictures on the market.

    (c) I returned later than my brother.

    (d) You (Vd.) went to the pictures.

    (e) Did you (tú) meet your friend?

    (f) We sat down on a bench.

    (g) The students obeyed at once.

    (h) The children got up early.

    (i) The guide showed us the interior of the convent.

    (j) I looked for a telephone.

3. Write down a telephone conversation between a Spaniard and his wife. The husband tells his wife that he will not be home at the usual time as he is going to the football match with some friends.

4. Finish the sentences with a few words of your own:

    (a) No aprende el español . . .

    (b) En el Rastro se venden . . .

    (c) Nunca leo tales . . .

    (d) Los niños cantaron . . .

    (e) Se fue pero volvió al cabo de . . .

5. Make up sentences using:

    sino   preocuparse   tal   resultar   pasar

6. In each group of words say which one, grammatically speaking, is the odd one out and give your reason.

    (a) deber   conocer   aprender   meter

    (b) mano   queso   libro   primo

    (c) entender   preferir   aprender   merendar

    (d) útil   hábil   mal   natural

    (e) poder   jugar   costar   poner

    (f) Televisión   programa   curiosidad   leche

    (g) su   mi   tu   nos

    (h) ferrocarril   postre   catedral   dentista

    (i) venir   pedir   vestir   decir

    (j) muchos   anchos   tantos   pocos

LECCION 17

¡OLE!

A las cinco y media de la tarde Robert y un grupo de veinte turistas llegaron a **la plaza de toros** en la Calle Alcalá, que se llama Plaza Monumental. Como el guía sacó **ayer** las entradas, billetes de **papel** verde con **la palabra** «sombra» en letras negras, pudieron entrar en seguida. Siguieron a Robert hasta los bancos de piedra.

—Qué **suerte tenemos** de no estar al sol!—dijo Robert— pero vale la pena **alquilar un cojín** porque estos bancos no son cómodos.

Los ingleses se sentaron en sus cojines y pusieron **los bolsos** y las máquinas en el suelo. Aunque nadie lo dijo entonces, **se sintieron** un poco nerviosos.

—¡Mirad aquellas mujeres españolas! exclamó una de las cuatro profesoras. —Robert ¿por qué llevan **mantillas**?

—Porque es **una corrida benéfica**. Algunas llevan **claveles** en el pelo también. En las corridas **corrientes** no se peinan **así**. Menos mal que vinieron Vds. hoy.

A las cinco y media en punto **sonó un clarín** y entraron **las cuadrillas** para **el paseíllo bravo**, los tres **matadores** vestidos con sus **trajes de luces**, la música **alegre**.

Luego salieron el primer toro y **los toreros** con **capotes** amarillos y color rosa.

Empezaron las tres **suertes** de **la faena**; primeramente, **los picadores** montados a caballo, segundo, **los banderilleros** ágiles y, tercero, el matador que hizo **unos pases hermosos**.

¡Olé! ¡Olé! ¡Olé!

Pero cuando el matador pidió **la muleta** y **la espada** de **acero** todo el mundo **se calló**. Fue la hora de la verdad. El matador puso la espada hábilmente, y murió el toro.

¡Olé!

Los aficionados sacaron los pañuelos y le dieron al valiente matador **una oreja** del toro.

95

—¿Les gusta su primera corrida?—preguntó Robert.
A las mujeres, no. Dijeron que es **un deporte** cruel.
Algunas quisieron salir. A los hombres, sí. Contestaron
que no es deporte sino arte o espectáculo.
Nunca está de acuerdo la gente sobre el tema de los toros.

VOCABULARIO

A.

el acero	the steel
alegre	gay
alquilar	to hire
así	thus, like that
ayer	yesterday
el bolso	the handbag
bravo	spirited, brave
callarse	to be quiet
el clarín	the trumpet
el clavel	the carnation
el deporte	the sport
la espada	the sword
hermoso	beautiful
la oreja	the ear
la palabra	the word
el papel	the paper
sonar(ue)	to sound
vestido	dressed

B. At the Bullfight:

el banderillero	the one who places darts in the bull's neck
el capote	bullfighter's large silk cape
la corrida de toros	the bullfight
la corrida benéfica	the charity bullfight
la cuadrilla	team of bullfighters under a matador
la faena	the task of fighting and killing the bull
la mantilla	the veil, head-shawl
el matador	the chief bullfighter
la muleta	bullfighter's small woollen cape
olé	bravo

el pase   the pass with the cape
el paseíllo   opening procession of all taking part
                           in the bullfight
el picador   horseman armed with a lance
la plaza de toros   the bullring
la suerte   phase of the bullfight
el torero   the bullfighter
el traje de luces   the suit of lights, i.e. suit decorated
                           with gold thread and semi-
                           precious stones

C. Expression:
   tener suerte   to be lucky

GRAMATICA

66. Irregular Preterites.

ANDAR	DAR	DECIR
anduve *I walked*	di *I gave*	dije *I said, I told*
anduviste	diste	dijiste
anduvo	dio	dijo
anduvimos	dimos	dijimos
anduvisteis	disteis	dijisteis
anduvieron	dieron	dijeron

ESTAR	HACER	PODER
estuve *I was*	hice *I did, I made*	pude *I could*
estuviste	hiciste	pudiste
estuvo	hizo	pudo
estuvimos	hicimos	pudimos
estuvisteis	hicisteis	pudisteis
estuvieron	hicieron	pudieron

PONER	QUERER	SABER
puse *I put*	quise *I wanted, I loved*	supe *I knew*
pusiste	quisiste	supiste
puso	quiso	supo
pusimos	quisimos	supimos
pusisteis	quisisteis	supisteis
pusieron	quisieron	supieron

TENER	TRAER	VENIR
tuve *I had*	traje *I brought*	vine *I came*
tuviste	trajiste	viniste
tuvo	trajo	vino
tuvimos	trajimos	vinimos
tuvisteis	trajisteis	vinisteis
tuvieron	trajeron	vinieron

67. **Preterite of Radical-Changing Verbs** ending in **-ir.**
Radical-changing verbs of ALL GROUPS which also end in -IR undergo a vowel change in the 3rd PERSON of the preterite.

Examples:

DORMIR *to sleep*	PREFERIR *to prefer*	PEDIR *to ask for*
dormí	preferí	pedí
dormiste	preferiste	pediste
durmió	prefirió	pidió
dormimos	preferimos	pedimos
dormisteis	preferisteis	pedisteis
durmieron	prefirieron	pidieron

Similarly:	*Similarly:*	*Similarly:*
morir *to die*	divertirse *to enjoy oneself*	elegir *to choose*
	sentirse *to feel*	reír *to laugh*
		repetir *to repeat*
		seguir *to follow*
		servir *to serve*
		vestir *to dress*

EJERCICIOS

1. Put the bracketed verbs into the preterite:
   - (a) ¿Dónde (poner) yo el bolsillo?
   - (b) Ellos (sentarse) en el suelo.
   - (c) ¿Qué (decir) el profesor?
   - (d) El viejo (morir) ayer.
   - (e) Ellos (leer) el telegrama a las ocho.
   - (f) Tú (pedir) más pan.
   - (g) El camarero (traer) el vino.
   - (h) ¿A qué hora (salir) Vds?

   (i) Vd. lo (hacer) en seguida.

   (j) ¿Por qué no (venir) vosotros?

2. Translate into Spanish:

   (a) She telephoned me at ten o'clock but I wasn't in.

   (b) The child wanted to get the tickets.

   (c) We read the newspapers as soon as we got up.

   (d) You (tú) hired a car (un coche).

   (e) "I bought the carnations in Toledo" said the lady.

   (f) That day we were very lucky.

   (g) When did you go to the bullfight?

   (h) I didn't know at that moment although I know now.

   (i) Children, why did you ask for the money?

   (j) Who gave the bullfighter the sword?

3. Answer the questions in Spanish:

   (a) ¿Cuántos ingleses fueron a la corrida?

   (b) ¿Dónde está la Plaza Monumental?

   (c) ¿Por qué alquilaron cojines?

   (d) ¿A qué hora empezó la corrida?

   (e) ¿Qué pasó primeramente?

   (f) ¿Cuándo se callaron los aficionados?

   (g) ¿Cómo puso el matador la espada?

   (h) ¿Por qué le dieron al matador la oreja?

   (i) ¿Qué dijeron las señoras inglesas sobre la corrida?

   (j) ¿Qué les contestaron los señores?

4. Each of the following words has more than one meaning. For each word write two sentences to illustrate the different meanings.

    pasar   suerte   sentir   sobre   querer

5. Replace the blanks with suitable Spanish words:

    Robert — las entradas en la —. Los ingleses alquilaron — porque — bancos no son —. Robert dijo — se llevan mantillas solamente en una corrida —. — las cinco y media en — sonó un — y — la corrida. Durante la tarde —seis toros. Unas — dijeron — es un deporte cruel — los hombres — — que no es deporte — un arte.

LECCION 18

EL MEDICO SE CALLA

—¡Qué vista tan espléndida! Tenemos suerte que está tan clara.

El grupo inglés acabó de llegar a Navacerrada, **lugar** popular en invierno para **esquiar** y de donde se ve una vista magnífica de **ambas** Castillas, Castilla la Vieja y Castilla la Nueva.

Los ingleses entraron en el hotel moderno para tomar café antes de irse al Real Sitio de **la Granja** de San Idelfonso, otro palacio **del estilo** francés con hermosos jardines. Mientras Robert y los mayores miraban **los tapices** dentro del palacio, Bill llevó a los niños a jugar cerca de las fuentes. Pero no había agua.

Merendaron en los jardines y después, mientras **descansaban** a la sombra, Robert les explicó el resto del itinerario.

—Siempre tenía ganas de conocer Segovia por su arquitectura—dijo el señor Brown.

—Pues, vamos—dijo Bill.

Al cabo de una hora estuvieron en aquella ciudad histórica en la cual vivieron los romanos durante trescientos años. En Segovia hay que ver el acueducto romano que traía—y todavía trae—agua a esta alta y aislada capital durante diecisiete siglos.

Los futbolistas **no tenían afición a** la historia y se sentaron a la sombra en un café. Les gusta más beber cerveza que ver muchas iglesias históricas. No querían ver **ni** otra plaza mayor **ni** otra catedral pero fueron con los demás para mirar el alcázar desde cuyas **torres** hay una vista panorámica de la meseta central.

Por desgracia ocurrió un accidente en el alcázar. El doctor Scott se cayó **peldaños** abajo y se **hizo daño en la pierna.** Peter y Philip le **ayudaron** hasta el autocar y, **a pesar de** sus protestas, Bill le condujo a **una casa de socorro. Una enfermera reconoció** la pierna y dijo que no tenía nada

grave. Le puso **un vendaje** y le **mandó** descansar durante
una semana. El médico **estuvo para** decir —Eso es imposible
—cuando pensó en las veces en que él mandaba descanso,
igualmente imposible, a sus pacientes, y se calló.

VOCABULARIO

A.
ambos	both
ayudar	to help
la casa de socorro	the first aid post
lo, los demás	the rest, remainder
descansar	to rest
la enfermera	the nurse
esquiar	to ski
el estilo	the style
la granja	the farm
el lugar	the place
mandar	to order
el peldaño	the step
la pierna	the leg
reconocer	to examine
el tapiz	the tapestry
la torre	the tower
el vendaje	the bandage

B. Expressions:
a pesar de	in spite of
estar para	to be about to
hacer daño a	to hurt
no tener afición a	to have no use for
por desgracia	unfortunately

C. Another Negative:
ni . . . ni	neither . . . nor

GRAMATICA

68. **The Imperfect Tense.**
The imperfect tense is used to express HABITUAL and
CONTINUOUS actions in the past, often translating the

English *used to, was . . . ing, were . . . ing,* or describing a state of indefinite duration.

The regular imperfect endings are as follows:

(1) **-ar verbs**

Mandar   *to order*

mandaba   I ordered, I was ordering
mandabas
mandaba
mandábamos
mandabais
mandaban

(2) **-er and -ir verbs**

Beber   *to drink*

bebía   I drank, I was drinking
bebías
bebía
bebíamos
bebíais
bebían

Vivir   *to live*

vivía   I lived, I was living
vivías
vivía
vivíamos
vivíais
vivían

69. **Había.** Había *there was, there were* is the imperfect of **hay.**

70. **Another Irregular Preterite.**

Conducir   *to drive*

conduje
condujiste
condujo
condujimos
condujisteis
condujeron

71. **El cual.**

The variable relative pronoun **el cual, la cual, los cuales, las cuales,** meaning *which* or *who,* may be used instead of **que** to avoid ambiguity.

Examples:
Los libros en la mesa los cuales compré ayer son para ti.
There can be no doubt that the masculine plural **los cuales** refers to the books and not to the table.
Se vende un piso en la calle en la cual vivía Ricardo.
Similarly the feminine **la cual** must refer to the street and not the flat.

72. **Cuyo.**
The relative adjective **cuyo** meaning *whose* is also variable; **cuyo, cuya, cuyos, cuyas.** Notice that it agrees with the noun it qualifies and NOT with the possessor.

Examples:
La mujer cuyo hijo murió ayer está en el hospital.
The woman whose son died yesterday is in the hospital.
En las montañas hay un castillo desde cuyas torres se ve la ciudad.
In the mountains there is a castle from whose towers one can see the city.

EJERCICIOS

1. Put the bracketed verbs into the imperfect tense:
   (a) El hombre (vivir) muchos años en España.
   (b) Mis amigos siempre (querer) ir a Londres.
   (c) Cada día vosotros (salir) a las nueve.
   (d) Yo (estudiar) el alemán en el colegio.
   (e) Tú (trabajar) en una agencia de viajes.
   (f) ¿(Aprender) Vd. el ruso?
   (g) Todos los días los abuelos (descansar) después de comer.
   (h) Siempre (llegar) Vds. a las cuatro en punto.
   (i) Ayer (hacer) mucho frío.
2. Translate the sentences into Spanish, choosing between the preterite and imperfect tenses.
   (a) Yesterday I received a letter from Spain.
   (b) The teacher used to speak to us about the history of the country.
   (c) I knew her in Madrid.

8

(d) "Why were you talking?" asked the teacher.
(e) The cousins wrote to each other every month.
(f) The guide arrived while the tourists were resting in the shade.
(g) I was looking at the tapestries when he spoke to me.
(h) Every winter they skied at Navacerrada.
(i) From time to time we spent a week in Segovia.
(j) We went down in the lift at once.

3. Pair the phrases from lists A and B to form complete sentences, taking particular note of the verb tenses.

A	B
Cada día los niños	merendaron en los jardines.
A las siete Juan	hacía mucho calor.
El jueves los turistas	jugaban en el parque.
—¿Cómo te llamas?—	no entendía el español.
Todos los días Rita y yo	llegábamos a las ocho.
Hoy	no aprendían el francés.
Los estudiantes	preguntó el profesor.
Tú	llueve.
Por desgracia el médico	fuiste al cine.
Mientras estábamos en Avila	llegó a la estación.

4. Translate into Spanish:
   (a) The teacher whose students were speaking listened carefully.
   (b) There were many people in the first aid post.
   (c) The driver at once drove him to a hospital.
   (d) I like neither sweets nor chocolates.
   (e) He asked for a book about the Romans that he wants to study.
   (f) I'm sorry but I am just about to go out.
   (g) In spite of being so cold it was very sunny.
   (h) The soldiers went to the palace.
   (i) Mr. Brown has no use for modern architecture.
   (j) Unfortunately, when you (Vd.) fell there was nobody to help you.

5. Construct sentences using:
   lo(s) demás; ni . . . ni; cuyo; a pesar de; estar para.

LECCION 19

MADRID DE NOCHE

Era de noche. En las calles bien iluminadas del centro de Madrid la gente todavía paseaba, las mesas en **las aceras** delante de los cafés estaban todas ocupadas y en las plazas los niños jugaban mientras los padres descansaban y **tomaban el fresco.**

Por las ventanillas de su autocar los turistas ingleses veían todo con interés. Iban a **una sala de fiestas y por eso** todo el mundo estaba muy elegante.

—Janet quería venir conmigo—dijo la señora Brown a la señora Scott.

—Morag también. No sé cuantas veces decía «llévame contigo» pero, **desde luego,** es **demasiado** tarde.

Los dos chicos irlandeses acompañaban a los mayores pero los demás niños se quedaron en el hotel. Se **acostaron** después de cenar y **una camarera** se encargó de cuidarlos.

En el «**Biombo Chino**» todo el mundo se divertía. **Bailaban,** tomaban «champán» español y «Cuba libre», charlaban y miraban el excelente espectáculo de **bailes** flamencos. Los hombres bailaban vestidos con trajes muy **ajustados** y las mujeres llevaban los trajes típocos con **volantes.** Los bailes eran animados y, por **el son** de **las castañuelas** y **el taconeado,** bastante **ruidosos.**

Al terminar su solo el bailador principal **tiró** a la joven señora Hilton **una flor** blanca. Ella la cogió y se la puso en su pelo **rubio.**

—No, mujer—le dijo el señor Reilly—hay que llevarla **junto al corazón,** así.

Los ingleses aplaudieron y el bailador **guapo** la tiró un beso con la mano.

Media hora más tarde el grupo salió para la «Taberna **Gitana**» para escuchar **el cante** flamenco. Había mucha gente, en la taberna, la mayoría extranjera, hacía mucho calor y **alguien fumaba** una pipa de fuerte olor. Sin embargo, el cante era emocionante.

Los ingleses se quedaron mucho tiempo. Al fin Robert se dio cuenta de que faltaban pocos minutos para las tres. Casi no podían creerlo.

VOCABULARIO

A.

la acera	the pavement
acostarse	to go to bed
ajustado	tight-fitting
alguien	somebody
bailar	to dance
el baile	the dance
el beso	the kiss
el biombo	the screen
la camarera	the chambermaid
el cante	the singing
las castañuelas	the castanets
el corazón	the heart
demasiado	too
desde luego	of course
encargarse	to take charge
la flor	the flower
fumar	to smoke
el gitano	the gypsy
guapo	handsome
el olor	the smell
rubio	fair, blonde
ruidoso	noisy
la sala de fiestas	the night club
el son	the sound
el taconeado	the heel tapping
tirar	to throw
el volante	the frill

B. Expressions:

junto a	next to
por eso	for that reason
tomar el fresco	to take the air

GRAMATICA

73. **Irregular Imperfects.**
Only three verbs are irregular in the imperfect tense.

Ir		**Ver**	
iba	*I went, I was going*	veía	*I saw, I used to see*
ibas		veías	
iba		veía	
íbamos		veíamos	
ibais		veíais	
iban		veían	

Ser
era   *I was*
eras
era
éramos
erais
eran

74. **Pronouns after Prepositions.**
Normally the forms used after prepositions are mí, ti, él, ella, Vd., nosotros, vosotros, ellos, ellas, Vds.

Examples:

El regalo es **para ti.**   The present is *for you.*
No me gusta ir **sin ellos.**   I don't like going *without them.*

However, after the pronoun **con** *with* the following singular forms are used: **conmigo** *with me*, **contigo** *with you* and **consigo** *with himself, herself, etc.*

Examples:

Viven conmigo.   They live with me.
No fuimos contigo.   We didn't go with you.

75. **Faltar** *to lack.* The construction is the same as for **gustar** *to like.*

Examples:

A Paco no le faltan amigos.   Paco doesn't lack friends.
Dígame si le hace falta   Tell me if you lack any-
   alguna cosa.   thing at all.

76. Por and Para.

Both of these words have various uses. As both of them can translate *for* it is important to distinguish between them.

Para indicates PURPOSE and DESTINATION while **por** indicates REASON and EXCHANGE.

Note:

Para

Comemos para vivir.	We eat (in order) to live.
¿A qué hora sale el tren para Londres?	What time does the train for London leave?
Hay un paquete para Vd.	There is a parcel for you.
¿Para qué sirve esto?	What is this for?

Expression:

Están para entrar.	They are just about to enter.

Por

¿Por qué lo hizo?	Why did he do it?
Lo hizo porque es tan pobre.	He did it because he is so poor.
Por eso tango que ir.	For that reason I have to go.
Gracias por su carta.	Thank you for your letter.
Está en Suiza por la salud.	He is in Switzerland on account of his health.
Me dio la pelota por el fusil.	He gave me the ball in exchange for the gun.
La novela escrita por Pío Baroja es muy interesante.	The novel written by Pío Baroja is very interesting.
El guardia corrió por la calle.	The policeman ran along the street.
No lo tire por la ventana.	Don't throw it through the window.

Expressions:

por la mañana, por la tarde	in the morning, in the afternoon
por ejemplo	for example
por supuesto	of course

EJERCICIOS

1. Insert **por** and **para**:
   (a) Fui a Segovia — ver el acueducto romano.
   (b) Los viajeros pasan — Francia.
   (c) Lo compré — cincuenta pesetas.
   (d) Date prisa, están — salir.
   (e) Tiene que estudiar mucho — los exámenes.
   (f) Aquí está una mesa libre — Vds.
   (g) Gracias — su carta que recibí ayer.
   (h) ¿Dónde está el autobús — Toledo?
   (i) El acueducto sirve — traer agua a la ciudad.
   (j) Siempre iba — la mañana.

2. With reference to the lesson, say whether the statements are correct or incorrect.
   (a) Los madrileños se acuestan temprano.
   (b) Los ingleses fueron a la sala de fiestas en autocar.
   (c) Todos los niños acompañaban a los padres.
   (d) La recepcionista cuidaba a los niños.
   (e) Todo el mundo se divertía en el «Biombo Chino».
   (f) Un bailador tiró una flor a una mujer española.
   (g) Los bailes flamencos eran animados.
   (h) Los turistas fueron a la «Taberna Gitana» para ver baile flamenco.
   (i) Había muchos extranjeros en la taberna.
   (j) Los ingleses volvieron al hotel a las dos.

3. Translate into Spanish:
   There were many foreigners in the night club besides the group who went with Robert. The Irish couple, whose two sons were with them, enjoyed every minute of the flamenco show. The boys laughed when one of the dancers threw a carnation to their mother. However, she picked it up and took it with her when they left for the gypsy tavern. They did not return to their hotel until three o'clock but there were still many people in the streets. The people of Madrid do not go to bed early.

LECCION 20

HASTA LA VISTA

Al día siguiente los Reilly no se levantaron hasta las once. Por eso tuvieron que desayunar en un pequeño café enfrente del Hotel Santo Domingo. Volvieron inmediatamente para **hacer las maletas** y dejar sus habitaciones libres al **mediodía.** Tiraban a las maletas, **blusas, camisas, corbatas, pantalones, calcetines, ropa interior, medias, toallas, perchas, joyas** y otros efectos. **Cerraron** las maletas **con llave** y las pusieron en el pasillo. Metieron en dos **cestas** nuevas los regalos y recuerdos, se lavaron las manos y la cara y, a pesar de **dejar caer** la cesta en la cual estaban las botellas de coñac, bajaron a tiempo para **almorzar** con los otros a la una y salir para Zaragoza a las dos menos cuarto. **¡Qué lástima despedirse** de Madrid!

El viaje a Zaragoza era bastante largo pero los ingleses miraban el paisaje y **escuchaban** la radio y el **tiempo pasó volando.** Al llegar a la antigua ciudad al borde del río Ebro, el autocar se **paró** delante de la **Residencia Puente, frente al ayuntamiento.** Bill se fue al garaje para **echar gasolina** y Robert condujo a los otros por la puerta giratoria hasta la recepción. Aunque pasaron sólo una noche allí, tuvieron que llenar un formulario: **apellido, nombres, fecha de nacimiento,** domicilio, nacionalidad y número del pasaporte.

Por la mañana salieron temprano y por la tarde pasaron la frontera. **Tardaban** dos días en **atravesar** Francia antes de llegar a Le Havre desde donde **cruzaron La Mancha** en barco, para desembarcar en Southampton. Luego viajaron juntos en su autocar hasta Manchester y entonces llegó la hora de despedirse. ¡Qué lástima, depués de **disfrutar** tanto tiempo todos **juntos!**

—Hace solamente tres semanas que nos conocimos—dijo el señor Evans. —**Apenas** lo creo.

—No se preocupen—le contestó Robert —Vamos a reunir aquí en Manchester, en enero.

Los turistas dieron las gracias al guía y al conductor y, un grupo **tras** otro, se fueron **a** su **casa**.

—Adiós, hasta la vista—dijo todo el mundo.

—Hasta enero.

—Hasta la reunión. Adiós, adiós.

VOCABULARIO

A.
almorzar (ue)	to lunch
el apellido	the surname
apenas	hardly, scarcely
atravesar(ie),	to cross
el ayuntamiento	the town hall
la blusa	the blouse
el calcetín	the sock
la camisa	the shirt
la cesta	the basket
la corbata	the tie
cruzar	to cross
despedirse	to say goodbye, to take one's leave
disfrutar	to reap benefit from
escuchar	to listen to
la fecha de nacimiento	the date of birth
frente a	facing
las joyas	the jewellery
junto	together
la media	the stocking
el mediodía	midday
el nombre	the name
el pantalón	the (pair) of trousers
parar	to stop
la percha	the hanger
la ropa interior	the underwear
tardar	to linger, to tarry
la toalla	the towel
tras	after, behind

B. Expressions:

a casa home (when movement is indicated)

cerrar con llave	to lock (to close with key)
dejar caer	to drop (to let fall)
echar gasolina	to fill up with petrol
el tiempo pasa volando	time flies
hacer las maletas	to pack the cases
¡qué lástima!	what a pity!

C. La Mancha   the English Channel
La Residencia Puente   the Bridge Hotel

GRAMATICA

77. **Hace, desde in Expressions of Time.**

(a) **Hace** with the preterite tense is translated as *ago*.

Examples:
Murió hace muchos años. *He died many years ago.*
Desembarcaron hace media hora. *They disembarked half an hour ago.*

(b) **Hace que** with the PRESENT tense is translated as *for* with the perfect tense.

Examples:
Hace tres años que vivo en el extranjero. *I have lived abroad for three years.*
Hace mucho tiempo que lo conozco. *I have known him for a long time.*

(c) **Desde** with the PRESENT tense and a date in the past is translated as *since* with the perfect tense.
Examples:
Trabajo aquí desde 1958. *I have worked here since 1958.*

PRUEBA

1. Put in the missing words, choosing from those in brackets:
    (a) El coche (es, está) en la calle.
    (b) Muchas gracias (por, para) las postales.
    (c) Los niños se lavan (los, las, sus) manos.
    (d) Ella dice que los zapatos negros son (suyos, suyas).
    (e) No nos (gusta, gustan) el edificio moderno.

(f) ¿De quién es (ese, ése) libro?

(g) Los turistas están (por, para) pasar la frontera.

(h) (Mira, Mire) Vd. el río.

(i) No es mío (pero, sino) suyo.

(j) Hace una semana que (llego, llegó) aquí.

2. Correct the sentences, each of which contains one mistake.

(a) Todos los días ella salió con una cesta enorme.

(b) ¿Adonde van los estudiantes?

(c) El profesor habla el alemán.

(d) Ven el matador célebre.

(e) Me gusta vino.

(f) Viajan por Inglaterra y Irlanda.

(g) Vivían en la grande casa en la plaza.

(h) ¿Ves ése pueblo en la sierra?

(i) No tengo una maleta grande.

(j) Trabajaba en el banco desde 1940.

3. Translate into Spanish:

(a) It isn't worth the trouble.

(b) She says he is lucky and I agree.

(c) The children are cold.

(d) My head aches and I am hot.

(e) English is spoken here.

(f) One must visit the Prado.

(g) What is your surname?

(h) What is the hotel like?

(i) I know the girl whose name is Francisca.

(j) They didn't realise I knew how to ski.

4. Fill in the blanks, choosing (a) between **ser** and **estar** and
   (b) between preterite and imperfect:

(a) A las diez ella — en el comedor.

(b) Durante tres siglos los romanos — en España.

(c) ¿Cómo — la noche, clara u oscura?

(d) La familia siempre — muy contenta.

(e) — mi amigo, Jaime, que me telefoneó.

(f) Cuando — pequeños vivíamos en Aranjuez.

(g) Todos los días la recepcionista — en su sitio.

(h) ¿Quién — el guía?

(i) ¿Dónde — los estudiantes durante el mes de agosto?

(j) Los hijos del médico — muy guapos.

REUNION

El Hotel Midland en Manchester. Sábado, el día dos de enero del año siguiente. Las cuatro de la tarde. Hay niebla y hace mucho frío. Por eso faltan ocho personas.

La sra. Evans: ¡Qué lástima! Los Reilly y los dos matrimonios jóvenes no están.

La sra. Brown: ¿Y dónde están los futbolistas?

Robert: Acaban de llegar después de jugar en el partido. Aquí están. Hola, Philip. Hola, Peter. ¿Qué tal el partido hoy? ¿Ganasteis?

Philip: Horrible. No había goles. Los que veían el balón no veían adonde meterlo.

Bill: *Lleva dos cervezas.* Tomad.

Peter: Gracias. No me gusta el invierno. Tengo ganas de estar de nuevo en España.

El Dr. Scott: Sí. Tenemos que pensar en el verano que viene.

La sra. Scott: Nosotros queremos ir a otra parte de España.

Robert: Bill y yo vamos a acompañar las excursiones a Andalucía; una semana en Sevilla, otra en Granada.

La srta. York: Dicen que:
Quien no ve Sevilla
no ve maravilla.

El sr. Brown: Entonces, ¿quién va a Sevilla? Dos, cuatro, cinco, diez, quince. . . .

SPANISH-ENGLISH VOCABULARY

a, at, to
abajo, below, down, downstairs
el abanico, fan
abierto, open
abrir, to open
el abuelo, grandfather
aburrido, boring
acabar de, to have just
la acera, pavement
el acero, steel
acostarse(ue), to go to bed
el acuerdo, agreement; estar de —,
to agree
además, besides
¿adónde? where to?
la aduana, Customs
el aficionado, amateur, fan, support-
er; no tener afición a, to have
no use for
afortunadamente, fortunately
agrícola, agricultural
el agua (f.), water
ahora, now; — mismo, right now,
this very minute
el aire, air, wind; al — libre, in the
fresh air
aislado, isolated
ajustado, tight-fitting
el alcázar, castle, fortress
alegre, gay, merry
alemán, German
la alfombra, carpet
algo (pron.), something, anything;
(adv.) rather, somewhat
alguien, anybody, anyone, somebody, someone
alguno, any, some
el almacén, (department) store, ware-
house
almorzar(ue), to lunch
alquilar, to let, hire, rent
alto, high, tall
allí, there
amarillo, yellow
ambos, both
el amigo, friend
amurallado, walled
ancho, wide
andar (irr.), to go (mechanically),
to walk
antes (adv.), before(hand); — de,
(prep.) before
la anticipación, anticipation; con —,
in advance

la antigüedad, antique
antiguo, ancient, antique, old
el año, year
el apellido, surname
apenas, hardly, scarcely
aprender, to learn
aprovechar, to take advantage of
aquel (adj.), that (over there);
aquél (pron.), that one (over there)
aquí, here
el árbol, tree
el arco, arch
el armario, cupboard, wardrobe
arriba, above, upstairs
el ascensor, lift
así, in that way, so, thus
atravesar(ie), to cross
aun, even, yet
aún (adv.), yet
aunque, although
el autobús, bus
el autocar, coach
la avenida, avenue
ayer, yesterday
ayudar, to help
el ayuntamiento, town hall
azul, blue

el bailador, dancer
bailar, to dance
el baile, dance, dancing
bajar, to come down, get down, go
down, take down
el banco, the bank; the bench, seat
bañarse, to bathe, to have a bath
el baño, bath
barato, cheap
la barca, small boat
el barco, boat
la basílica, basilica (cathedral)
bastante, enough, fairly, quite (a
lot)
beber, to drink
belgo, Belgian
bello, beautiful, fine
benéfica, charitable
el beso, kiss
la biblioteca, library
bien, well
el billete, banknote, ticket; — de ida
y vuelta, return ticket
el billetero, wallet
el biombo, screen
blanco, white

la **blusa,** blouse
el **bocadillo,** sandwich
el **bollo,** roll
el **bolso,** handbag
 bonito, nice, pretty
 bordado, embroidered
la **botella,** bottle
el **brazo,** arm
 bueno, good
 buscar, to look for

el **caballo,** horse; **a —,** on horseback
la **cabeza,** head
el **cabo,** end; **al — de,** after (a period
 of time)
 cada, each
 caer (irr.), to fall
el **café,** cafe, coffee
 caído, fallen
la **caja,** box; **la cajita,** small box
el **calcetín,** sock
 caliente, hot, warm
el **calor,** heat; **hacer —,** to be hot
 callar, to keep silence
la **calle,** street
la **cama,** bed
la **camarera,** chambermaid, waitress
el **camarero,** waiter
 cambiar, to change, exchange
el **camino,** way; **de —,** on the way
la **camisa,** shirt
 cansado, tired
 cantar, to sing
el **cante,** singing
la **cara,** face
el **caramelo,** toffee
 caro, dear, expensive
la **carretera,** highway, main road
la **carta,** letter
el **cartel,** poster
la **casa,** house; **la — de socorro,**
 first-aid post; **en —,** at home;
 ir a —, to go home
las **castañuelas,** castanets
 castellano, Castilian
la **catedral,** cathedral
 celebrar, to celebrate
 célebre, celebrated, famous
la **cena,** supper
 cerca (de), near (to)
la **cerilla,** wax match
 cerrado, closed, shut
 cerrar(ie), to close, shut; **cerrar
 con llave,** to lock
el **cerro,** hill
la **cerveza,** beer
la **cesta,** basket
 ciego (adj.), blind; **el ciego,** blind
 man

el **cigarrillo,** cigarette
el **cine,** cinema
la **circulacion,** movement of people
 and traffic
la **ciudad,** city, large town
el **clarín,** bugle, trumpet
 claro, clear; of course
el **clavel,** carnation
el **clima,** climate
la **cocina,** kitchen; **la — eléctrica,**
 electric cooker
el **coche,** car
 coger, to gather, to grasp, to hold,
 to take hold of
el **cojín,** cushion
el **colegio,** (private) school
el **comedor,** dining-room
 comer, to eat, to have dinner
 como, as, like; **¿cómo? how?;
 ¿cómo es?** what is it like?
 cómodo, comfortable
 completamente, completely, fully
 comprar, to buy; **ir de compras,**
 to go shopping
 comprender, to understand
 con, with; **conmigo,** with me;
 contigo, with you (fam.); **consigo,** with himself, herself, etc.
el **conde,** Count
 conducir, to drive, to lead
el **conductor,** driver
 conocer, to be acquainted, to know
el **conserje,** concierge, janitor
 contento, content, glad
 contestar, to answer
el **corazón,** heart
la **corbata,** tie
 corregir, to correct
 correr, to run
la **corrida** (de toros), bullfight
 corriente, common, current, ordinary, regular
 corto, short
la **cosa,** thing
la **costumbre,** custom
 creer, to believe, to think
la **crema bronceadora,** suntan cream
la **cruz,** cross
 cruzar, to cross
el **cuadro,** picture
 ¿cuál?, which (one)? (rel. pron.)
 el —, etc., which
 cualquiera, any (at all)
 cuando, ¿cuándo?, when
 cuanto, ¿cuántos?, how much,
 how many?
el **cuarto,** quarter; room; **el — de
 baño,** bathroom; **el — de estar,**
 living room; **cuarto,** fourth

el **cucurucho,** cone-shaped paper bag
la **cuenta,** account; **darse — de,** to
  realise
el **cuidado,** care; **tener —,** to be
  careful, to take care
cuidar, to look after
el **cumpleaños,** birthday
la **curiosidad,** curio; curiosity
cuyo, whose

charlar, to chat
el **chico,** boy, lad
chino, Chinese
el **churro,** a kind of fritter
chutar, to shoot (a goal)

el **daño,** harm; **hacer —,** to hurt
dar (irr.), to give; **— a,** to give
  onto; **— de comer,** to feed;
  — una vuelta, to take a turn
de, from, of; **de nuevo,** again
debajo de, under
deber, must, ought; **el —,** duty
decir (irr.), to say, to tell
dedicado, dedicated
dejar, to leave (behind); **— caer,**
  to drop
delante de, in front of
el **delantero,** forward (football)
lo, los demás, the rest
dentro, inside
el **deporte,** sport
desayunar, to have breakfast
descansar, to rest
desde, from, since; **— luego,** of
  course
la **desgracia,** misfortune; **por —,**
  unfortunately
despedirse, to say goodbye; to
  take one's leave
despertar(ie), to awaken, to rouse
  from sleep; **— se,** to wake up
después, afterwards; **— de,** after
detrás (de), behind
el **día,** day; **de —,** in the daytime
el **diente,** tooth
difícil, difficult
Dios, God; **— mio!,** good heavens!
disfrutar, to profit by; to reap the
  benefit from
divertirse, (ie) to enjoy oneself, to
  have a good time
dolerse(ue), to ache; **me duele la
  cabeza/la garganta,** I have a
  headache/sore throat
el **domicilio,** home (address)
donde, ¿dónde?, where
dormir(ue), to sleep

la **duda,** doubt; **sin —,** without doubt
durante, during, for

e, and (used before **i** and **hi —**
  except **hie**)
echar, to throw, throw away, throw
  out; **— una carta,** to post a
  letter; **— gasolina,** to fill up
  with petrol
el **edificio,** building
el **ejemplo,** example; **por —,** for
  example
elegir(i), to choose
la **Embajada,** embassy
emocionante, impressive
empezar(ie), to begin, start
en, at, in, into, on, onto
encantador, charming, delightful,
  enchanting
encargarse, to take charge
encontrar(ue), to find, to meet
la **enfermera,** nurse
enfermo, ill
enfrente (de) opposite (to)
enseñar, to show, to teach
entender(ie), to understand
el **entierro,** burial
entonces, then
la **entrada,** entrance, ticket
entre, among, between
los **entremeses,** hors-d'oeuvre
el **equipo,** team
la **escalera,** staircase, stairs
el **escaparate,** shop window
escribir, to write
escuchar, to listen (to)
eso (neuter), that (one); **por —,**
  for that reason
la **espada,** sword
España, Spain
español, Spanish
el **espectáculo,** show
esperar, to hope; to expect; to
  wait (for)
esquiar, to ski
la **estación,** season; station
el **estadio,** stadium
el **estanco,** state-controlled shop, sel-
  ling monopolies such as tobacco
el **estanque,** artificial lake
estar (irr.), to be; **— para,** to be
  about to
este (adj.), this; **éste** (pron.), this
  one
el **estilo,** style
estrecho, narrow
estrenar, to show, wear for the
  first time
el **estudian te,** student

la **faena**, task
la **falda**, skirt
la **falta**, foul (football), mistake
faltar, to be lacking
favor, por —, please
la **fecha**, date
feliz, happy
el **ferrocarril**, railway
la **ficha**, token
la **flor**, flower
el **formulario**, form
francés, French
frente a, facing
fresco, cool, fresh; **tomar el —**, to take the air
el **frío**, cold; **hacer —**, to be cold
la **fuente**, dish; fountain
fuera (de), outside
fuerte, strong
fumar, to smoke
el **fusil**, gun, rifle
el **futbolista**, footballer

ganar, to earn, to gain, to win
ganas, tener — de, to feel like, to desire
la **garganta**, throat
la **gasolina**, petrol; **echar —**, to fill up with petrol
la **gente**, people
giratorio, revolving
el **gitano**, gypsy
el **globo**, balloon
el **gol**, goal
golpear, to beat, to knock
las **gracias**, thanks; **muchas —**, thank you very much
grande, big, great
la **granja**, farm
grave, grave, serious
gritar, to shout
guapo, handsome
la **guerra**, war
el **guía**, guide
gustar, to like, to please

hábilmente, cleverly
la **habitación**, bedroom, room
hablar, to speak, to talk
hacer (irr.), to do, to make; **hace mucho tiempo**, a long time ago
el **hambre** (f.), hunger; **tener —**, to be hungry
hasta, as far as, until; **— la vista**, until we meet again; **— luego**, until later
hay, there is, there are; **— que**, one must
el **hermano**, brother

hermoso, beautiful
el **hijo**, son
el **himno**, hymn
holandés, Dutch
el **hombre**, man; **¡hombre!** exclamation of surprise
la **hora**, hour, time
hoy, today
el **huevo**, egg

la **iglesia**, church
iluminado, illuminated, lit
importar, to matter, **no importa**, it doesn't matter
infierno, hell
Inglaterra, England
inglés, English
interesar(se), to be interested in, to interest
interrumpir, to interrupt
el **invierno**, winter
ir (irr.), to go; **— a**, to be going to; **— se**, to go away
irlandés, Irish
la **isla**, island

el **jabón**, soap
el **jamón**, ham
el **jardín**, garden
el **jerez**, sherry
joven, young
la **joya**, jewel; **las joyas**, jewellery
jugar(ue), to play
el **juguete**, toy
junto, together; **— a**, next to

el **lago**, lake
largo, long
lástima, ¡qué —!, what a pity, shame!
lavar(se), to wash; **lavar y marcar**, shampoo and set
leer, to read
lejos (de), far (from)
lentamente, slowly
levantarse, to get up
la **libra**, pound
libre, free
el **libro**, book
el **limón**, lemon
el **limpiabotas**, shoe or bootblack
limpio, clean
luego, later, then
el **lugar**, place
la **luz**, light

llamar, to call; to knock; **llamarse**, to be called (named)
la **llave**, key

llegar, to arrive
llenar, to fill
llevar, to carry, to take, to wear

la **madre,** mother
madrileño, inhabitant of Madrid
la **madrugada,** dawn
madrugar, to get up early
mal, badly; **malo,** bad
la **maleta,** suitcase; **hacer una —,** to pack a case
malgastador, wasteful
la **Mancha,** the English Channel
mandar, to command, order, send
la **mano,** hand
el **mantel,** tablecloth
la **mantequilla,** butter
la **mantilla,** veil
mañana, tomorrow; **la —,** morning; **por la —,** in the morning
la **máquina,** machine; **la — (fotográfica),** camera
maravillar, to admire; **-se,** to marvel, wonder at
el **marido**, husband
marrón, brown
más, more, most
el **matrimonio,** married couple
(el) **mayor,** bigger, biggest; elder, eldest
la **media,** stocking
medio, half
el **médico,** doctor
mejor, better, best
menor, less, least; smaller, smallest; younger, youngest
menos, minus; **las cuatro — diez,** ten to four; **menos mal,** all the better, a good thing
el **mercado,** market
merecer, to deserve, merit
merendar(ie), to take afternoon tea, to have a picnic meal or a snack
la **merienda,** afternoon tea, picnic meal, snack
la **mermelada,** jam
el **mes,** month
la **mesa,** table
la **meseta,** plateau
meter, to put
mientras, while
mirar, to look at, to watch
mismo, same, very; **lo —,** the same thing
la **montaña,** mountain
montar, to rise (a horse)
morir(ue), to die
el **mueble,** piece of furniture; **los muebles,** furniture

la **mujer,** wife; woman
la **muñeca,** doll; wrist
la **muralla,** city wall
muy, very

el **nacimiento,** birth
nada, nothing
nadar, to swim
nadie, nobody, no one
la **naranja,** orange; **de color —,** orange coloured
necesitar, to require
negro, black
ni (siquiera), not even; **ni . . . ni,** neither . . . nor
la **niebla,** fog, mist
ninguno, none, not any
el **niño,** boy, child
la **noche,** night; **de —,** at night
el **nombre,** name
norte, north
nuevo, new
el **número,** number
nunca, never

obedecer, to obey
la **obra,** work
ocupado, busy, occupied
ocurrir, to happen, to occur
el **oficio religioso,** religious service
oir (irr.), to hear, to listen; **— misa,** to hear Mass
el **ojo,** eye
¡olé! bravo
la **oreja,** ear
el **oro,** gold
oscuro, dark
el **otoño,** autumn
otro, another, other

el **padre,** father, parent
pagar, to pay (for)
el **país,** country
el **paisaje,** landscape
la **palabra,** word
palmadas, dar —, to clap
el **pan,** bread
el **pantalón,** (pair of) trousers
el **pañuelo,** handkerchief, headscarf
el **papel,** paper
el **paquete,** packet, parcel
para, (in order) to; for (destination)
parar, to stop
parecer, to appear; to seem
el **pariente,** relation
la **parte,** part; **¿de — de quien?** on whose behalf?
el **partido,** match
el **pasajero,** passenger

9

pasar, to happen; to pass; to spend (time)
pasear, to (take a) walk
el paseillo, parade
paseo, dar un —, to go for a walk
el pasillo, passage
el pastel, cake
pedir(i), to ask for
peinarse, to comb one's hair
el peldaño, step, stair
la película, film, picture
el pelo, hair
la pelota, ball
la peluquería, hairdressing salon
el peluquero -a, hairdresser
pena, merecer la —; valer la —, to be worth the trouble
peor, worse, worst
pequeño, small
la percha, coathanger
perezoso, lazy
el periódico, newspaper
pero, but
la persiana, window blind
pesar, a — de, in spite of
el peso, weight
el pie, foot; ir a —, to go on foot
la piedra, stone
el pintor, painter
la pipa, pipe
la piscina, swimming pool
el piso, flat, floor, storey
la plata, silver
el plato, plate; de segundo —, for second course
la plaza, square; la — de toros, bullring
pobre, poor
poco, little
poder (irr.), to be able
poner (irr.), to put; ponerse, to become, to put on (clothes)
por, along, by, for, on account of, through; — ¿que? why?; — supuesto, of course
porque, because
el portal, entrance, main door(way)
la postal, postcard
el postre, dessert
precioso, exquisite, beautiful
preciso, exact, precise
preguntar, to ask (a question); —se, to wonder
preocupar(se), to worry
la primavera, spring
primero, first
el primo, cousin
la princesa, princess
el príncipe, prince

prisa, darse — to hurry; de —, quickly
el profesor, teacher
pronto, soon
la propina, tip
propio, own
proteger, to protect
el pueblo, village, small town
el puente, bridge
la puerta, door
el puesto, stall
el punto, dot, point; en —, on the dot

que (rel. pron.), that; ¿qué? what?
quedar, to remain, stay, to be left
querer (irr.), to love, want
el queso, cheese
quien, ¿quién? who
quitarse, to take off

el rascacielos, sky-scraper
el rato, while; pasar el —, to pass the time
la raya, stripe
real, real, royal
recibir, to receive
reconocer, to examine
el recuerdo, souvenir
el regalo, gift, present
reír(i), to laugh
el reloj, clock, watch
repetir(i), to repeat
la residencia, hotel
responder, to reply
la respuesta, reply
resultar, to turn out
la revista, magazine
el rey, king
rico, rich
el río, river; situado al borde del —, on the river
rodeado, surrounded
rojo, red
la ropa, clothing, clothes; la — interior, underwear
la rosa, rose; de color —, pink
rubio, blonde, fair
ruidoso, noisy
ruso, Russian

saber (irr.), to know (facts), to know how; ya sabes, you know very well
sacar, to take out
la sala, drawing-room, hall, parlour; la — de fiestas, nightclub
salir (irr.), to go out, to leave
la salud, health
salvo, safe

sano, healthy; — y salvo, safe and sound
el santo, saint
la sed, thirst; tener —, to be thirsty
seguida, en —, at once
seguir(i), to continue, to follow
segundo, second
seguramente, probably, surely
el sello, stamp
la semana, week
sentarse(ie), to sit down
sentir(se)(ie), to feel, to regret; lo siento, I'm sorry
el señor, gentlemen, Mr., sir
la señora, lady, Mrs., madam
la señorita, young lady, miss
ser (irr.), to be
si, if, whether
sí, yes
siempre, always
el siglo, century
siguiente, following, next
la silla, chair
sin, without
sino, but
el sitio, place
sobre, on (top of); — todo, above all
el sobrino, nephew
el socorro, aid, help, succour
el sol, sun; tomar el —, to sunbathe
solamente, only
el soldado, soldier
sólo, only; solo, alone
la sombra, shade, shadow
el sombrero, hat
el son, sound
sonreír, to smile
soñar(ue), to sound
sorprender, to surprise
subir, to ascend, climb, come up, get on, go up
sucio, dirty
el suelo, floor, ground
el sueño, dream; tener —, to be sleepy
la suerte, luck; phase of the bullfight; por —, luckily; tener —, to be lucky

taconear, to tap with the heels
tal, such a
la talla, size
también, also
tan, so; tan . . . como, as . . . as
tanto, tantos, so much, so many
el tapiz, tapestry
la taquilla, ticket office
tardar, to be long, delay, linger

la tarde, afternoon, evening; por la —, in the afternoon, evening; tarde (adv.), late
el té, tea
el teatro, theatre
el teléfono, telephone; llamar por —, to call by telephone
temprano, early
tener (irr.), to have, possess; — que, to have to
tercero, third
terminar, to end, finish
tiempo, time; weather; mucho —, a long time; el — pasa volando, time flies
la tienda, shop
el tío, uncle
tirar, to fire, pull, toss, throw
la toalla, towel
el tocador, cloakroom, dressing table
todavía, still, yet
todo, all, everything; todos, all, everybody; — el mundo, everybody
tomar, to take
el torero, bullfighter
el toro, bull
la torre, tower
trabajador, hard-working
trabajar, to work; — mucho, to work hard; sin —, without exertion
traer (irr.), to bring
el traje, dress, suit; el — de luces, bullfighter's richly embroidered suit
tranquilamente, calmly, quietly
el tranvía, tram
tras, after, behind
travieso, mischievous, restless
el tren, train
la trucha, trout
la tumba, tomb

u, or (used before o or ho)
único, only, single, unique

vacilar, to hesitate
vacío, empty
la valla, fence, stockade
el valle, valley
varios, several, various
el vendaje, bandage
vender, to sell
venir (irr.), to come
la ventana, window; ventanilla, small window esp. of vehicles
ver (irr.), to see
el verano, summer

la **verdad**, truth; ¿(no es) **verdad?**
   isn't it, won't it? etc.
verde, green
la **vergüenza**, shame
el **vestido**, dress, frock; **vestido con,**
   dressed in
vestir(i), to dress, to wear
la **vez**, occasion, time; **una —**, once;
   dos veces, twice; **de — en**
   cuando, from time to time; **en —**
   de, instead of
viajar, to travel
el **viaje**, journey

viejo, old
el **vino**, wine
vivir, to live
el **volante**, frill
volver(ue), to return
la **vuelta**, return; **dar una —**, to take
   a turn (round the block)

y, and
ya, already, now

el **zapato**, shoe

ENGLISH-SPANISH VOCABULARY

able, hábil; to be —, poder (irr)
about, de, sobre
abroad, en el extranjero
accident, el accidente
to accompany, acompañar
to ache, doler (ue)
address, la dirección, el domicilio
to admire, admirar, maravillar
advance, adelante; in —, con
   anticipación
advantage, la ventaja; to take —
   of, aprovechar
after, al cabo de, después de; tras
afterwards, después
afternoon, la tarde
again, de nuevo
agency, la agencia
agile, ágil
ago, hace
to agree, estar de acuerdo
agricultural, agrícola
air, el aire; fresh —, el aire libre;
   to take the —, tomar el fresco
to allow, dejar, permitir
along, por
already, ya
also, también
although, aunque
always, siempre
American, americano
among, entre
angel, el ángel
another, otro
to answer, contestar
antique, la antigüedad; antiguo
any, alguno; — at all, cualquiera
anybody, alguien
aqueduct, el acueducto
anything, algo, cualquier cosa
to applaud, aplaudir
arch, el arco
architect, el arquitecto
architecture, la arquitectura
arm, el brazo
to arrive, llegar
art, el arte
as, como; as . . . as, tan . . . como
to ask, preguntar; to — for, pedir (i)
aspirin, la aspirina
at, a, en
aunt, la tía
autumn, el otoño
avenue, la avenida

bad, malo
badly, mal
balcony, el balcón
ball, el balón, la pelota
balloon, el globo
bandage, el vendaje
bank, el banco
bar, el bar
basket, la cesta
bath, el baño; —room, el cuarto
   de baño; to have a —, bañarse
to be, estar (irr.), ser (irr.); to be
   about to, estar para
beautiful, bello, hermoso, precioso
because, porque
bed, la cama; to go to —, acostarse
   (ue)
bedroom, la habitación
beer, la cerveza
before, (adv.) antes; (prep.) antes de
to begin, empezar (ie)
behind, detrás (de)
Belgian, belgo
to believe, creer
bench, el banco
besides, además (de)
best, el mejor
better, mejor
between, entre
big, grande; —ger, más grande,
   mayor
birth, el nacimiento
birthday, el cumpleaños
black, negro
blind, ciego; window —, la
   persiana
blond, rubio
blouse, la blusa
blue, azul
boat, el barco; small —, la barca
book, el libro
boot, la bota; —black, el limpiabotas
boring, aburrido
both, ambos
bottle, la botella
box, la caja
boy, el chico, el niño
brandy, el coñac
brave, bravo, valiente
bread, el pan
breakfast, el desayuno; to have —,
   desayunar

123

bridge, el puente
to bring, traer (irr.)
brother, el hermano
brown, marrón
bugle, el clarín
building, el edificio
bull, el toro
bullfight, la corrida (de toros)
bullfighter, el torero
bullring, la plaza de toros
burial, el entierro
bus, el autobús
but, pero, sino
butter, la mantequilla
to buy, comprar
by, por

café, el café
cake, el pastel
to call, llamar; to be —ed, llamarse
camera, la máquina (fotográfica)
can, poder (irr.)
capital (city), la ciudad
car, el coche
care, el cuidado; to take —, tener
    cuidado
carnation, el clavel
carpet, la alfombra
castanets, las castañuelas
Castilian, castellano
castle, el alcázar, el castillo
cathedral, la basílica, la catedral
catholic, católico
centre, el centro
century, el siglo
chair, la silla
chambermaid, la camarera
to change, cambiar
charge, la carga; to take —,
    encargarse
charitable, benéfica
charming, encantador
to chat, charlar
cheap, barato
cheese, el queso
chemist's, la farmacia
child, el niño
Chinese, el chino
to choose, elegir (i)
church, la iglesia
cigarette, el cigarrillo
city, la ciudad
to clap, dar palmadas
clean, limpio
clear, claro
clever, hábil, inteligente
climate, el clima
clock, el reloj
to close, cerrar (ie)

closed, cerrado
clothes, la ropa; under—, la ropa
    interior
coach, el autocar
coathanger, la percha
coffee, el café
cold, el frío; to be — (weather),
    hacer frío; (people), tener frío
colour, el color
to comb (one's hair), peinarse
to come, venir (irr.); to — down,
    bajar; to — up, subir
comfortable, cómodo
completely, completamente
concierge, el conserje
content, contento
to continue, seguir (i)
convent, el convento
to correct, corregir
country, el país
couple (married), el matrimonio
cousin, el primo
to cross, atravesar (ie), cruzar
cross, la cruz
cruel, cruel
cupboard, el armario
curio, la curiosidad
cushion, el cojín
custom, la costumbre
Customs, la aduana

to dance, bailar
dance, dancing, el baile
dancer, el bailador
dark, oscuro
date, la fecha
daughter, la hija
dawn, la madrugada
day, el día
dear (beloved), querido; (expen-
    sive), caro
to decide, decidir
dedicated, dedicado
dentist, el dentista
department store, el almacén
to deserve, merecer
to desire, tener ganas
dessert, el postre
to die, morir (ue)
difficult, difícil
dining room, el comedor
dirty, sucio
to disembark, desembarcar
to distribute, distribuir
to do, hacer (irr.)
doctor, el doctor, el médico
doll, la muñeca
door, la puerta; main —, el portal
dot, el punto; on the —, en punto

doubt, la duda; without —, sin
   duda
down(stairs), abajo
drawing room, la sala
dream, el sueño
to dress, vestir(se) (i); el traje, el
   vestido; —ed in, vestido con
dressing table, el tocador
to drink, beber
to drive, conducir
driver, el conductor
to drop, dejar caer
during, durante
Dutch, holandés

each, cada
ear, la oreja
early, temprano; to get up —,
   madrugar
easy, fácil
to eat, comer
effect, el efecto
egg, el huevo
elegant, elegante
embassy, la embajada
embroidered, bordado
empty, vacío
England, Inglaterra
English, inglés
enough, bastante, suficiente
to enter, entrar (en)
enthusiasm, el entusiasmo
to enjoy oneself, divertirse (ie)
enormous, enorme
even, (adv.) aun; (adj.) igual; not
   —, ni (siquiera)
evening, la tarde
everybody, todo el mundo, todos
exact, exacto
to examine, reconocer
to exclaim, exclamar
excursion, la excursión
exertion, el esfuerzo; without —,
   sin esfuerzo, sin trabajo
to explain, explicar
exquisite, precioso
eye, el ojo

face, la cara
facing, frente a
to fall, caer (irr.)
fallen, caído
family, la familia
famous, célebre, famoso
fan, el abanico; el aficionado (del
   fútbol)
fantastic, fantástico
far, lejos; as — as, hasta
farm, la granja

father, el padre
to feed, dar de comer
to feel, sentir(se) (ie)
fence, la valla
to fill, llenar
film, la película
to find, encontrar (ue)
to finish, terminar
first, primero; — aid post, casa
   de socorro
floor, el suelo; (storey), el piso
flower, la flor
fog, la niebla
to follow, seguir (i)
foot, el pie; to go on —, ir a pie
football, el fútbol
footballer, el futbolista
for, durante, para, por
foreigner, el extranjero
form, el formulario
fortress, el alcázar
forward (football), el delantero
foul, la falta
fountain, la fuente
fourth, cuarto
France, Francia
free, libre
French, francés
fresh, fresco
friend, el amigo
frill, el volante
from, de, desde
front, la frente; in — of, delante de
frontier, la frontera
fruit, la fruta
function, la función
furniture, los muebles; piece of —,
   el mueble

garage, el garaje
garden, el jardín
gay, alegre
German, alemán
to get, obtener (irr.), ponerse (irr.); to
   — down/off, bajar; to — onto,
   subir; to — up, levantarse
to give, dar (irr.); to — onto, dar a
glad, alegre, contento
to go, ir (irr.); to — away, irse; to
   be going to, ir a; to — down,
   bajar; to — out, salir (irr.); to
   — up, subir
goal, el gol
God, Dios
gold, el oro
good, bueno; — heavens! ¡caramba! ¡Dios mío!
goodbye adiós; to say —, despedirse

grandfather, el abuelo
to grasp, coger
green, verde
group, el grupo
guide, el guía
gun, el fusil
gypsy, el gitano

hair, el pelo; —dresser, el peluquero; —dresser's, la peluquería
half, medio
ham, el jamón
hand, la mano
handbag, el bolso
handkerchief, el pañuelo
handsome, guapo
to happen, ocurrir, pasar
happy, feliz
hardly, apenas
hard-working, trabajador
hat, el sombrero
to have, tener (irr.); to — just, acabar de; to — no use for, no tener afición a; to — to, tener que
head, la cabeza
health, la salud
healthy, sano
to hear, oír (irr.)
heart, el corazón
heat, el calor
hell, el infierno
to help, ayudar
help, el socorro
here, aquí
to hesitate, vacilar
high, alto
hill, el cerro
to hire, alquilar
to hold, coger
home, la casa; at —, en casa; to go —, ir a casa
hors d'oeuvre, los entremeses
horse, el caballo; on —back, a caballo
hot, caliente; to be —, (weather) hacer calor, (people) tener calor
hotel, el hotel, la residencia
house, la casa
how? ¿cómo?; — much? ¿cuánto?
hunger, el hambre (f); to be hungry, tener hambre
to hurry, darse prisa; to be in a —, tener prisa
to hurt, hacer daño
husband, el marido
hymn, el himno

if, si
ill, enfermo

immediately, inmediatamente
impressive, emocionante
in(to), en
industrial, industrial
inside, dentro
instead of, en vez de
to interest, interesar; to be —ed in, interesarse
interest, el interés
interesting, interesante
interior, el interior
to interrupt, interrumpir
itinerary, el itinerario
to invite, invitar
Ireland, Irlanda
Irish, irlandés
island, la isla
isolated, aislado
italian, italiano

jam, la mermelada
jewel, la joya
jewellery, las joyas
journey, el viaje

key, la llave
king, el rey
kiss, el beso
kitchen, la cocina
to knock, golpear, llamar
to know, conocer, saber (irr.); to — how, saber

lack, la falta; to be —ing, faltar
lady, la señora
lake, el lago; artificial —, el estanque
landscape, el paisaje
late, tarde; later, luego, más tarde
to laugh, reír (i)
lazy, perezoso
to lead, conducir
to learn, aprender
to leave, dejar, salir (irr.)
lemon, el limón
lemonade, la limonada
letter, la carta
library, la biblioteca
lift, el ascensor
light, la luz
to like, gustar
like, como; what is it —? ¿cómo es?
to linger, tardar
list, la lista
to listen, (to), escuchar, oír (irr.)
lit, iluminado
little, pequeño; poco
to live, vivir

to **lock,** cerrar con llave
long, largo; **to be —,** tardar
to **look (at),** mirar; **to — after,**
cuidar; **to — for,** buscar
to **love,** querer (irr.)
luck, la suerte; **—ily,** por suerte;
to be —y, tener suerte
to **lunch,** almorzar (ue)

madam, señora
magazine, la revista
magnificent, magnífico
to **make,** hacer (irr.)
man, el hombre
manicure, la manicura
many, muchos
map, el mapa
market, el mercado
Mass, la misa
match, (sport) el partido; **wax —,**
la cerilla
to **matter,** importar
to **meet,** dar con, encontrar (ue)
melon, el melón
memory, la memoria
military, militar
minus, menos
minute, el minuto
mischievous, travieso
Miss, señorita
Mr., el señor
Mrs., la señora
modern, moderno
moment, el momento
monastery, monasterio
month, el mes
monument, el monumento
more, más
morning, la mañana
most, el más
mother, la madre
mountain, la montaña
much, mucho
museum, el museo
music, la música
must, deber; **one —,** hay que

name, el nombre
narrow, estrecho
nationality, nacionalidad
naturally, naturalmente
near (to), cerca (de)
neither . . . nor, ni . . . ni
nephew, el sobrino
nervous, nervioso
never, nunca
new, nuevo
newspaper, el periódico
next, siguiente; **— to,** junto a

nice, bonito
niece, la sobrina
night, la noche
nightclub, la sala de fiestas
nobody, nadie
noisy, ruidoso
north, el norte
now, ahora, ya; **right —,** ahora
mismo
number, el número
nurse, la enfermera

to **obey,** obedecer
object, el objeto
occupied, ocupado
of, de; **— course,** desde luego, por
supuesto; **of course it is,** claro
que sí
old, antiguo, viejo; **—er,** más
antiguo/viejo, mayor
on(to), en; **— top of,** sobre
once, una vez; **at —,** en seguida
only, solamente, sólo; **the — one,**
el único
to **open,** abrir
open, abierto
or, o, u
orange, la naranja; **de color**
naranja
to **order,** mandar
ordinary, corriente
other, otro
ought, deber
outside, fuera
own, propio

packet, el cucurucho, el paquete
painter, el pintor
palace, el palacio
paper, el papel
parade, el paseíllo
parent, el padre
park, el parque
part, la parte
to **pass,** pasar
passage, el pasillo
passenger, el pasajero
passport, el pasaporte
patron, el patrón
pavement, la acera
to **pay (for),** pagar
people, la gente
perfumery, la perfumería
person, la persona
petrol, la gasolina; **to fill up with**
—, echar gasolina
photograph, la fotografía; **to take**
a —, sacar una fotografía

picnic meal, la merienda; **to have a —,** merendar (ie)
picture, el cuadro; **(film)** la película
pink, de color rosa
pipe, la pipa
pity, la piedad; **what a —!** ¡qué lástima!
place, el lugar, el sitio
plate, el plato
plateau, la meseta
to **play,** jugar (ue)
please, por favor; **to —,** gustar
poor, pobre
Portuguese, portugués
to **post,** echar
postcard, la postal
poster, el cartel
pound, la libra
to **prefer,** preferir (ie)
present, el regalo
pretty, bonito
prince, el príncipe
princess, la princesa
probably, probablemente, seguramente
problem, el problema
to **profit by,** disfrutar
programme, el programa
to **prohibit,** prohibir
to **protect,** proteger
protest, la protesta
protestant, el protestante
to **put,** meter, poner (irr.); **to — on (clothes),** ponerse; **to — put on for the first time,** estrenar

quarter, el cuarto
quiet, callado, tranquilo; **—ly,** tranquilamente; **to be —,** callar (se)
quite, bastante

radio, la radio
railway, el ferrocarril
rather, algo
to **read,** leer
to **realise,** darse cuenta (de)
to **receive,** recibir
reception, la recepción
receptionist, la recepcionista
red, rojo
to **regret,** sentir (ie)
relation, el pariente
religious, religioso
to **repeat,** repetir (i)
replica, la réplica
reply, la respuesta
to **require,** necesitar

to **respond,** responder
to **rest,** descansar
rest, el descanso; **lo, los demás,** el resto
restaurant, el restaurante
to **return,** volver (ue)
revolving, giratorio
rich, rico
to **ride,** montar
river, el río; **on the River . . .,** situado al borde del río . . .
road, la carretera
roll, el bollo
Roman, romano
room, el cuarto, la habitación; **living —,** el cuarto de estar
royal, real
to **run,** correr
Russian, ruso

safe, seguro; **— and sound,** sano y salvo
saint, el santo
same, mismo
sandal, la sandalia
sandwich, el bocadillo
satisfied, satisfecho
to **say,** decir (irr.)
season, la estación
school, el colegio
screen, el biombo
sculpture, la escultura
second(ly), segundo
to **see,** ver (irr.)
to **seem,** parecer
to **sell,** vender
serious, grave
to **serve,** servir (i); **to — for,** servir para
service, (religious) el oficio religioso
several, varios
severely, severamente
shade, la sombra
shame, la vergüenza
to **shampoo and set,** lavar y marcar
sherry, el jerez
shirt, la camisa
shoe, el zapato
to **shoot (goals),** chutar
shop, la tienda; **to go —ping,** ir de compras
short, corto
to **shout,** gritar
to **show,** enseñar
silver, la plata
to **sing,** cantar
singing, el cante
sister, la hermana

to **sit,** sentarse (ie)
situated, situado
size, (clothes) la talla, **(shoes)** el número
to **ski,** esquiar
skirt, la falda
sky-scraper, el rascacielos
to **sleep,** dormir (ue); **to be —y,** tener sueño
slowly, lentamente
small, pequeño; **—er,** más pequeño, menor
to **smile,** sonreír
to **smoke,** fumar
snack, la merienda; **to have a —,** merendar (ie)
so, así; **tan; — much,** tanto
soap, el jabón
sock, el calcetín
soldier, el soldado
some, algunos, unos
somebody, alguien
something, algo, alguna cosa
somewhat, algo
son, el hijo
soon, pronto
sorry, miserable; **I am —,** lo siento
to **sound,** sonar (ue)
sound, el son
souvenir, el recuerdo
Spain, España
Spanish, el español
to **speak,** hablar
to **spend, (money)** gastar, **(time)** pasar
spite, la malevolencia; **in — of, a** pesar de
splendid, espléndido
sport, el deporte
spring, la primavera
square, la plaza
stadium, el estadio
staircase, stairs, la escalera
stall, el puesto
stamp, el sello
station, la estación
to **stay,** quedar
steel, el acero
step, el peldaño
still, todavía
stocking, la media
stone, la piedra
to **stop,** parar
street, la calle
stripe, la raya
strong, fuerte
student, el estudiante
style, el estilo
such, tal

suit, el traje
suitcase, la maleta; **to pack a —,** hacer una maleta
summer, el verano
sun, el sol; **to —bathe,** tomar el sol
suntan cream, la crema bronceadora
supper, la cena; **to have —,** cenar
surname, el apellido
to **surprise,** sorprender
surrounded, rodeado
sweater, el sueter
to **swim,** nadar; **swimming pool,** la piscina
sword, la espada

table, la mesa
tablecloth, el mantel
to **take,** llevar, tomar; **to — a turn (walk),** dar una vuelta; **to — down,** bajar; **to take off,** quitar; **to — out,** sacar
to **talk,** hablar
tall, alto
to **tap (with the heels),** taconear
tapestry, el tapiz
task, la faena
tavern, la taberna
tea, el té; **afternoon —,** la merienda
to **teach,** enseñar
teacher, el profesor
team, el equipo
telegram, el telegrama
telephone, el teléfono; **to call by —,** llamar por teléfono
terrace, la terraza
to **tell,** decir (irr.)
thanks, las gracias; **thank you,** gracias
that, ese; **— over there,** aquel; **eso; que**
theatre, el teatro
then, entonces, luego; pues
there, allí; **— is,** hay
thing, la cosa
to **think,** creer, pensar
third(ly), tercero
thirst, la sed; **to be —y,** tener sed
this, este; esto
throat, la garganta
through, por
to **throw,** tirar
thus, así
ticket, el billete, la entrada; **return —,** el billete de ida y vuelta; **— office,** la taquilla
tie, la corbata
tight-fitting, ajustado

time, la hora, el tiempo, la vez;
from — to —, de vez en cuando;
— flies, el tiempo pasa volando
tip, la propina
tired, cansado
to, a, hasta
tobacco, el tabaco
today, hoy
toffee, el caramelo
together, junto
tomorrow, mañana
token, la ficha
tomb, la tumba
tooth, el diente
tourist, el turista
towel, la toalla
tower, la torre
town, la ciudad, el pueblo
town hall, el ayuntamiento
toy, el juguete
traffic, el tráfico; la circulación
train, el tren
tram, el tranvía
to travel, viajar
tree, el árbol
trousers, el pantalón
trout, la trucha
trumpet, el clarín, la trompeta
truth, la verdad
to turn out, resultar
typical, típico

uncle, el tío
under(neath), debajo de
to understand, comprender, entender
(ie)
unfortunately, por desgracia
until, hasta
up(stairs), arriba
usual, usual

valley, el valle
various, varios
very, muy; — same, mismo
view, la vista
village, el pueblo
to visit, visitar

to wait (for), esperar
waiter, el camarero
to wake up, despertarse (ie)
to walk, andar; to go for a —, pasear
wall, la pared; city —s, las
murallas; —ed, amurallado
wallet, el billetero

to want, querer (irr.)
war, la guerra
wardrobe, el armario
warm, caliente
to wash, lavar(se)
wasteful, malgastador
watch, el reloj
water, el agua (f.)
way, el camino; on the —, de
camino
to wear, llevar
weather, el tiempo
week, la semana
weight, el peso
well, bien
what, lo que; ¿qué?
when, cuando; ¿cuándo?
where, donde; ¿dónde?; — to?
¿adónde?
whether, si
which, ¿cuál? el cual, que
while, mientras; el rato
white, blanco
who, ¿quién? que, quien
whose, cuyo; ¿de quién?
why, ¿por qué?
wide, ancho
wife, la mujer
to win, ganar
window, la ventana; — of vehicle,
la ventanilla; shop —, el escaparate
wine, el vino
winter, el invierno
with, con; — me, conmigo; — you,
contigo; — himself, consigo
without, sin
woman, la mujer
to wonder, preguntarse; to — at,
maravillarse de
wonderful, estupendo
word, la palabra
to work, trabajar
work, la obra, el trabajo
to worry, preocuparse
worse, peor
worst, el peor
to write, escribir

year, el año
yellow, amarillo
yes, sí
yesterday, ayer
yet, aún, todavía
young, joven; —er, más joven,
menor

INDEX TO GRAMMAR

Numbers in bold type refer to the chapters and numbers in ordinary type refer to sections. Letters refer to vocabulary notes.